MW00584475

Lessons
for Living

Lessons for Living

What Only Adversity
Can Teach You

Phil Stutz

RANDOM HOUSE

NEW YORK

Published in the United States by Random House,
an imprint and division of Penguin Random House LLC, New York.

RANDOM HOUSE and the HOUSE colophon are
registered trademarks of Penguin Random House LLC.

Most of the essays in this work were originally published in the
newsletter *A Real Life*.

Hardback ISBN 9780593731086
Ebook ISBN 9780593731093

Printed in the United States of America on acid-free paper

randomhousebooks.com

9 8 7 6 5 4 3 2 1

First Edition

Book design by Diane Hobbing

Dedicated to Barbara McNally,
who started it all

Contents

Introduction

Maybe you're here because you read *The Tools* or because you saw me in the Netflix documentary called *Stutz*. I've become known as the "psychiatrist to the stars," a descriptor that bothers me as much as it likely bothers you. The best thing I can do to refute that misconception is to tell you what I've learned as a psychiatrist over the last forty years. Along the way, with my partner, Barry Michels, I developed a new kind of psychotherapy. It differs from the old model in one crucial respect: it works.

I grew up in New York and I attended City College of New York and NYU medical school, which is where I received my medical and psychiatric training. After that, I was a prison psychiatrist at Rikers Island for five years, as well as carrying on a private practice. But I was becoming increasingly demoralized about the inability of psychiatry to really help patients.

A move to Los Angeles did nothing to make me more hopeful. I was still determined to find a better way, but with no one to turn to for advice, I felt rudderless. Out of pure stubbornness, I kept looking, anywhere and everywhere, for ideas, for answers, until I finally found them in the one group I never thought to search: my own patients.

I found that if I threw out the rule book and treated them with the respect any human being would want—rather than as a collection of genetic or psychological anomalies—they were willing to go wherever my instincts led me. This was fortunate because the only way to proceed was through trial and error. With my patients' encouragement, I began to develop something I called the Tools.

The Tools were very different from psychotherapy as it was practiced at that time. I had grown so frustrated because I felt as if traditional therapy was designed to make it impossible for patients to change. The patient was either trapped in a past that no longer existed or living in fantasy about a future that hadn't arrived yet—and might never. Only the Tools could open the door to the infinite wisdom of the present.

There were three qualities that identified someone that was in Tools therapy.

1. Homework: It is naïve to think your experience in a therapist's office is enough to change your life. Life isn't a static thing that you can cover over with a fresh coat of paint. Life is a process. If you want to change a process, you need to work on it daily.

2. Forward Motion: Old-school therapy kept you in the past. The highest value is placed on understanding what happened to you back then. When you use the Tools, the highest value is in taking the next step into your future.

3. Higher Forces: We are only a tiny part of an infinite universe. On our own we can do nothing. But, in a silent miracle, the universe puts its energies at the service of human evolution. This is most obvious when a person's life is falling apart (financial ruin, emotional rejection, low self-esteem, etc.). It's in desperation that we become willing to go beyond our limited view of the universe. If we don't recognize the presence of higher forces, they can't help us. We need to feel them in the present. The Tools give us the ability to embody higher forces.

Barry and I knew that this information was too important to keep to ourselves. Together we wrote *The Tools* and its follow-up, *Coming Alive*. Both of them were well received and opened the door to a wider audience. The books represented an approachable way to bring higher forces into our lives. But we also knew there was an aspect of the Tools that couldn't be conveyed in the how-to model those books were written to be. There was a whole other level to the concepts, but I couldn't figure out how to get it across.

Time passed.

One day, I was looking around my office and came upon a bunch of short essays I had written in the 1990s and early 2000s sitting on a shelf. I had written them after I had developed the Tools as a practice, but before Barry and I had written *The Tools* as a book. I had forgotten about them; they were essentially lost to time.

I had written them for a health and wellness newsletter called *A Real Life,* which was ahead of its time. This was pre-internet. The newsletter was an actual paper, locally distributed.

Its publisher, Barbara McNally, had been interested in my work and gave me the opportunity to write a column presenting some of my ideas. Each essay was about a common problem, like depression, rage, and loneliness. Finding them on my shelf, I remembered that the feedback we got from the newsletter readers, even those who devoured self-help books, was that these pieces felt like something totally new.

I realized that I needed to release them to a broader audience. Not only do they address the larger, deeper themes I was trying to get across, but they are even more relevant today than they were when I was writing them all those years ago.

Why?

Because the problems they address have gotten worse, not better. As a psychiatrist I see the effect of this worsening every day. The pandemic, the proliferation of social media, greed, the dysfunction of our divisive political system. All these things have made our sense of isolation even worse. It used to be that the patient would walk into my office and leave the world's problems outside until they were done talking about themselves. Now, the patient's personal problems have to stay outside and it's the world's problems that demand attention in session. This makes sense. It is no longer possible to believe that our personal problems don't impact the world, and vice versa. I expand on this phenomenon in the pages that follow.

(I should also mention that I went through the essays

and changed them so that they sit comfortably in today's world, which took shockingly little adjustment. Still, I don't think readers need to hear about my beeper going off.)

Therapy, without faith in higher forces, is likely to leave you feeling worse than before. Working on yourself doesn't have to be selfish. If you do, you have more energy, not less. That energy will transform the world.

This book shows you why and how.

Lessons
for Living

Just an Illusion

Our culture denies the nature of reality. It holds out a promise that you can live in an ideal world where things come easily, a world in which unpleasant experiences can be avoided, where there is never a lack of immediate gratification. Worse, it suggests that if you do not live in this world, something is wrong with you. This ideal world is a realm of illusion. No matter how promising this world seems, it does not exist.

Be honest. Your own life experiences have been far from ideal. But what you have experienced is what is real, not what you would like to experience. In short, the nature of reality is this:

- Life includes pain and adversity.
- The future is uncertain.
- Accomplishment of any kind requires discipline.
- You are not special. No matter what you do, you cannot avoid these aspects of life.
- This will never change.

There is love, joy, surprise, transcendence, and creativity as well, but these never occur separately from the above five points.

Yet there always seem to be others who are exempt from the adversity of daily living. The media portrays them to us. They are physically more perfect, they do not worry, they are certain of their course through life. They never lack for love or companionship. They are secure in themselves. These people seem to have abolished the negative aspects of life. And this power makes them special. Products are marketed with promises of putting us in this group. We all feel a pressure to convince others that we are part of it. This holds true for the poor kid unsure if dinner is coming and the billionaire with six homes. When everyone acts as if a fantasy is real, it begins to seem real.

But only for someone else. In your own life, you find yourself unable to take a risk. You don't know how to make a decision. Your financial future is uncertain. Your face has a new wrinkle. There is no time to parent properly. You simply cannot get life under control. There is nothing wrong with this. This is how it feels to be alive. The problem is that the other group has become the standard, and self-esteem starts to depend on being like them. An adverse event feels like something is happening that is not supposed to be happening. The natural experiences of living make you feel like a failure.

Is there another way? Can you live life with its conflicts, uncertainties, and disappointments and somehow feel good about yourself? You can. But it requires a completely new orientation. The first step is to realize that life is a process. Our culture leads us to forget this fact and makes the destructive suggestion that we can perfect life and then get it to stand still. The ideal world with the superior people is like a snapshot or a postcard. A moment frozen in time that never existed. But real life is a process, it has movement and depth. The realm of illusion is an image, dead and superficial. Still, these images are tempting. There is no mess in them.

How can you retrain yourself to prefer what is real and alive, although often painful? The key depends on a simple truth that we resist: life is made up of events. The only real way to accept life is to accept the events that comprise it. And the flow of events never stops. The driving force of the universe reveals itself via the events of our lives. Why resist this fact? Because it places us in a world that is not perfectible or predictable. There is awe and mystery in the fact that no one knows what will happen next. But it also makes us feel small and out of control. The realm of illusion suggests that we can get above this flow of events. But that would be a spiritual death, for it is only events that allow us to be in touch with an alive, meaningful universe. If fate is woven of a series of events, then mental health is the ability to accept our fate with enthusiasm.

Dealing with events is similar to being a good parent. It is not enough to just show up. You need a point of view and a set of tools. It is impossible to deal with events constructively without being prepared. Why are so few people prepared? Because they hope that the events, particularly the bad ones, will never come. They believe that the ideal world

is real, that they can live in a world of ease. They play the
lottery every day. In our culture, very few people prepare for
anything.

Preparing yourself with a philosophy enables you to
change the meaning of a negative event. With a specific philosophy, you can aggressively change your perception of
events. The philosophy of events is as follows.

- Adverse events are supposed to happen.
- Their existence doesn't mean there is
  something wrong with you.
- There is always an opportunity in a negative
  event.
- Developing spiritual skills is more important
  than getting a good result.

It is not possible to know what adversity you will face in
the future, but whatever it is—misunderstanding, abandonment, risk, conflict, loss—this philosophy helps you
not to be taken by surprise. It allows you the distance to
step back and label the event and give it value above and
beyond its immediate details. The event becomes generic.
Events of abandonment, for instance, will teach you to develop a set of skills that will make you more emotionally
independent. But if you fail to label an event, you can't see
the value in it. All you want is for it to be over. And once it
is over, you forget all about it. You learn nothing. Labeling

an event, even just to call it an adverse event, allows you to take advantage of it instead of it taking advantage of you.

It's best to think of the skills that events teach you as spiritual skills rather than psychological skills, which reminds you that it is a meaningful universe that touches you via the events of your life (particularly the adverse events). These spiritual skills help you relate to the universe by finding meaning in everyday events.

Try an experiment. Next time you face an adverse event, apply the philosophy of events. Observe how you feel. If you are open-minded and do this with regularity, you will begin to experience the first glimmer of higher meaning in events. Your experience will change. In training to make events your teachers, you make real experience the foundation of your philosophy.

That is the purpose of a human life.

Out of the Blues

Sometimes, as a doctor, it's harder *not* to give medicine. Once in a while, a patient will insist on being medicated, but for their own good, I must refuse. Used properly, antidepressants like Prozac can be a godsend, but in some cases, they are a cure that is worse than the disease. That would have been the case for Joe, a thirty-year-old English professor at an elite college. He was a charismatic teacher who lit up in the lecture hall and at social events. He was also developing into an accomplished fiction writer, with one bestseller already published. The problem was, left to his own devices, he would descend into a paralyzed funk and stay there until there was another lecture to give or book signing to attend. Weekends were bad and midterm breaks and summers were worse. His classic pose was slouched in front of the TV, the house in disarray, without the vaguest idea of how he was going to use the rest of the day. He was stuck somewhere between a lost child and a disillusioned old man, with his literary career about to come to a premature end. He had an almost comically distorted view of his situation. Every time the black mood hit, he would ask me, "Why now?" as if its appearance was a surprise. Then, on cue, he would plaintively ask when joy was going to come, as if it were Santa Claus or the Messiah. It would have been funny in a Woody Allen movie, but in real life it was a disaster in the making.

Despite his situation, I wouldn't put him on antidepressants. He tried whining, then begging. I was unmoved because his attitude toward medication stemmed from the very mindset that created the depression in the first place. That said, if your psychiatrist recommends you take medication, you should consider it seriously. Unlike in Joe's case, sometimes things are worse than they appear. But not for Joe. He would change for the better the moment he became honest about the illusion around which he had organized his life. Simply put, he believed that he could regulate his mood and his motivation through outer events. He wanted things outside himself, like alcohol, his students' applause, or fame, to put him in a positive state. He would brood about a college girlfriend with whom he'd had a sexually electric but dangerously unstable relationship, demanding to know when he'd be "in love" like that again. Love was one more thing to make him happy. He clearly saw Prozac in the same light.

Believing that things outside you will make you happy is false hope. The Greeks considered it the "doubtful gift of the gods." In reality, there can be only two outcomes. Either the hoped-for thing does not happen, or it does and its effect quickly wears off. Either way, you are worse off than before because you have trained yourself to fixate on outer results. An extreme example of this is found in *Man's*

Search for Meaning, written by Viktor Frankl, a psychiatrist who survived Auschwitz. In 1944, a rumor spread that the Allies would liberate the camp by Christmas. Christmas Day came and went but the troops were not to arrive for months. Frankl, who was the camp doctor, relates that he saw more deaths between Christmas and New Year's than at any time at the camp. He attributed this to the dashed hopes of the prisoners. As extreme as the circumstances were, Frankl insists he survived by developing inner tools to sustain his mood.

Just to say this plainly: human beings can never be made happy by the material world. We are spiritual beings and can be emotionally healthy only when we are in touch with a higher world. We need higher forces just as we need air. This is not abstract philosophy, it is a description of our nature. But it requires constant work to stay in touch with these forces. And yet it is also our nature to try to avoid this work. Thus we are prey to the illusion that we can remain spiritually passive because something outside us will restore our mood. Given this hope, depression can be understood as the failure of the outer world to take care of you. In that sense, it can be a great teacher.

Each time depression recurs, it is a reminder that you cannot rely on the outer world. This awareness is the first step in overcoming depression.

Once you give up hope that the outer world can regulate your mood, the only alternative is to maintain it yourself, regardless of outer conditions. Accepting this responsibility is the second step in fighting depression. Joe took absolutely no responsibility for the state he was in and wanted to use Prozac to continue that irresponsibility. The first time I suggested he could control how he felt by internal means he looked at me as if I were crazy. To be fair to him, our entire culture is based on using outer things to regulate our moods. Taking responsibility for how you feel isn't an intellectual decision. It requires monitoring yourself every moment. This is the most freeing thing a person can do, but also the most tedious. Your connection to the higher world must be won in a series of small moments. Each time you become demoralized, depressed, or inert, you must counteract it right then.

Like the holes in Swiss cheese, these black interludes are holes in our relation to life, places where our connection to the higher world is severed. Everyone has them to some degree or another. Even if we notice them, we don't feel the responsibility to do something to change our state. This is tragic, since these holes in our energy are huge opportunities to change the nature of our life force. The life force is actually a series of habits. If your habit is to look outside yourself for stimulation or validation, then each time you fail to get it, you'll become depressed. But if you assume inner responsibility for your own mood and take action to connect yourself to higher forces right at the moment you feel yourself going into the hole, you will develop habits that put you on a new level of energy and aliveness.

Even those who accept in principle that they must be responsible for their own moods tend not to do the work during their dark moments. They still lack a sense that it is possible to transform themselves out of a black mood using nothing but inner tools. This sense of possibility is essential to overcome depression. The only way to achieve this confidence is to take a tool and actually experience how it works. Only then will you be willing to do what is required, which is to use it over and over, sometimes many times within one day.

Here is one very effective tool that I call transmutational motivation. It helps you transmute negative emotions into pure motivation, a higher type of will that allows you to move forward in life. If you take the time to practice it, you'll see that it is possible to systematically change your mood.

Begin by feeling the heavy, demoralized feeling you have when depressed. Focus on it, and tell yourself that you are going to change that feeling into something positive. Imagine that, up above your head, there is a powerful flow of energy, a jet stream. Now picture yourself taking a specific action that represents forward motion in your life. It can be a risk, something you've avoided doing, or even some daily practice like writing, exercising, or meditating. Put this specific picture above your head in the jet stream. Now you are going to fly straight up into this picture by feeling yourself take that action and imagining that this feeling causes you to ascend. Tell yourself that nothing else matters except taking the action. As you feel yourself rise, sense that the world around you falls away. There is nothing except the action itself. Rise high enough to enter the picture. Once inside, tell yourself that you have a purpose. You will feel a powerful energy. To end the exercise, open your eyes and tell yourself that you are determined to take the pictured action. This time you will feel the picture above you pull you effortlessly up into itself. You will feel expanded and energized. Once you learn this, you can do the whole thing in fifteen seconds. But done consistently during your dark moments, you will begin the process of transforming your life force.

The Grateful Flow

Negative thinking is powerful. You start to worry about something. Or you feel the world is treating you unfairly. Your concerns seem rational at first, but in a few minutes, your mind is out of control. The thoughts pound away at you with a dark life of their own. "I know I'm going to lose my job. I'll be destitute. No one else will hire me." You are lost in a world of your own obsessions.

The thoughts hound you during the day, and wake you at 5:00 A.M. They can be unbearably painful, and almost impossible to stop. Your mind is broken. If you bought an appliance that worked this poorly you would be at the store demanding a refund. But there is no return policy for your brain.

Step back a minute, and consider these characteristics of negative thinking:

It's dynamic—negative thinking represents a force in your consciousness that wants to displace anything healthy.

It's irrational—the thoughts seem real when you're having them, but when you look back, they are almost always exaggerated or out of touch with reality.

It's a habit—and like all habits, the more you practice

negative thinking, the stronger it becomes and the harder it is to stop.

Yet, it is *your* mind, isn't it?

So, why should negative thinking be so hard to control?

The answer is that negative thinking is the expression of an inner adversary, and until you become aware of this adversary, you'll be powerless to defeat it. Think of your mind as a computer with a virus already built in. Until you find it, that virus will destroy everything else in the computer.

I call this inner adversary Part X. It is a part of your psyche, and it has an agenda all its own.

This inner demon is absolutely determined to keep you from experiencing a fact of reality—everything is always moving. Even the most materialistic view of the universe (theoretical physics) now accepts this. Every moment, including right now, you are floating in a world of movement. This is good news—the underlying movement makes the universe into one great organism, a dynamic organism that continuously produces new and surprising things. This ceaseless creativity makes the universe inherently positive and giving.

It is exactly this boundless, alive quality of the universe that Part X hates. This negative force wants something else, something it desires at all costs. *It wants to be special*. But there is no opportunity to be special when you are part of the moving, whole universe, since everything that happens in it is a product of that whole. Good things may come your way, you may succeed, but you did not make these things happen yourself. In a holistic universe, the individual is only part of the system; by himself he can do nothing. Specialness, on the other hand, requires the sense that you "did it yourself." Being special implies that you are not part of the system, that you can overcome a negative universe on your own. And so the ever-moving, ever-creating spiritual core of the universe—the force that connects everything—is the one thing that can deprive you of your "chance for specialness."

Part X wields a very potent weapon against this moving whole—your own thoughts. It creates negative thoughts and makes them so intense, so insistent, that they drown out any experience of the real world. You no longer respond to the world, you merely react to what X tells you about the world. Spiritually blinded, you are totally alone. The experience of the true universe, constantly creating and infinite in scope, can only be positive. But as long as you are caught in negativity, it is impossible to experience the positive feelings of wholeness inherent in an alive universe. It is as if it does not exist. Part X has shattered reality, and it has done so with your help.

Negative thinking can easily become a habit, mostly because negative thoughts become so familiar. We start to identify with negativity. Take a worrier, for example. When he thinks "I know I'm doomed," he is having a familiar experience. He's worrying. And he can create this experience for himself anytime. No matter how painful it may be, it feels familiar, it's home. His inner X will tell him, "This is the real you, don't fight it." And most of the time he won't.

To control this demon, you must find a force in your soul that is even stronger than the power of negative thinking. That force is gratefulness. Gratefulness appreciates the immediate experience of reality, replacing negative thoughts with thoughts about what's really going on. It alludes to things in your life that are solid and real, and implies that these things are products of the moving whole. Gratefulness creates the physical sensation of being in the immediate presence of a positive, giving spiritual force, and allows you to feel that you are part of the system again, no longer isolated.

Gratefulness differs from "positive thinking," which tends to focus on events that have not yet happened (with the hope that they will). The very nature of positive thinking is not grounded in reality. Think about it, have you ever been able to get yourself out of a deeply worried mood by thinking happy thoughts about your future? Not likely. What we all need is a way to penetrate the veil of negativity and connect to the moving force of wholeness as it exists right now. We need to get into the habit of grateful thinking, of letting grateful thoughts flow through our minds as our own defense against negative thinking.

———

Try this. For about thirty seconds, think of things for which you're grateful. Not just the big things; focus on everyday things that we often take for granted. "I am grateful I can see, I am grateful my children are healthy, I am grateful my car started today, I am grateful I had money to eat breakfast, I am grateful I have hot water, I am grateful I live in a democracy." Think of new things as much as possible—you'll soon see that even on your worst day, there are an infinite number of things already happening that are positive. And every one of these things has been given to you by the dynamic spiritual organism that underlies reality. It is always there. It is always creating. It is always stronger than Part X.

The power of this exercise is that you are teaching your mind to work in a new way. You are forcing your mind into a state of highly creative motion that is analogous to the underlying motion of the universe itself.

As the grateful thoughts well up, become aware of the energy inside yourself that is creating them. You start to feel one with the universe, and have a new confidence that you can control your mind. You have dissolved negative thoughts. And without realizing it, you have prepared yourself to pray. Not a specific form of prayer, and not necessarily connected to an organized religion. Independent of your personal spiritual beliefs and practices, you have led the mind beyond itself, making it a bridge into a higher place.

The Sky Is Falling

"The sky is falling! The sky is falling!" This is the iconic proclamation of Chicken Little spreading unwarranted panic throughout the land. In the fairy tale, the sky never fell. But could the "sky" actually be falling this time? Our symbolic sky—which we often think of as our societal safety net—is an umbrella of institutions that we rely on for our security. Here are just a few of them: corporate healthcare, the academic establishment, politics on every level, the financial engine, the armed forces, the judicial system, etc.

The safety net we've built is huge, and if it falls, we will lose the ability to live and work without fear. Unfortunately, it really does feel like it may be falling. If our collective mental health is any indicator, alarm bells have been sounding for a while now. Antianxiety medications are being prescribed at an alarming rate to little or no effect. Nobody can sleep, and this isn't your grandmother's insomnia. It's a whole new thing.

We all sense something is terribly wrong even though we can't see it. What we can see is the rage and confusion that accompany this cosmic struggle. It's natural for us to think of this as a battle against some evil antagonist bent on destroying us: Darth Vader back for another round. But the real adversary is someone much more dangerous—yourself.

This other side of yourself uses what may be the most unstoppable weapon of all: dissatisfaction. We live in a chronically dissatisfied world today because we no longer know how to be satisfied.

In a society where nobody is happy with what they have, there can be no harmony or peace of mind. All that remain are competitiveness and paranoia. When we don't have everything we want, we conclude that everyone else must be getting more than their fair share.

But the adversary isn't even the entirety of you. It's merely a part of you. Hence, as we described in the last chapter, its name: *Part X*.

Part X is much more than a concept. It's a real actor that commands its forces against you. It never gives up and is committed to destroying your potential. It is crucial that we know how to identify Part X when it is pursuing its job.

Here are four ways to identify an active Part X:

Primitive—Evolution requires movement. Part X keeps you in a state of comfort and familiarity. This may feel pleasant but there is no forward motion. You remain stuck in repetitive thinking or behaviors.

Reward (**Magical Reward**)—Part X claims that if you meet your goals, you will be magically fulfilled. This is a lie. Many successful people are deeply unhappy. They've achieved superficial goals that were all just false promises of satisfaction.

Injury—Part X perpetuates the sense that the whole world is against you. You hoard injuries to prove that life is unfair.

Must—Part X creates an energy that drives you to react on impulse. It presents things you feel you *must* do and cannot resist, even when they may not be good for you.

(I use the acronym PRIM as shorthand to describe these tendencies.)

To put it more simply, *Part X invents problems that we don't really have and creates solutions that only make those problems worse.* Whether it sets its sights on a career, a relationship, or a personal goal, Part X will do what it can to prevent you from feeling happiness.

But there's the paradox: problems are necessary for growth. Part X will weaken you, but it's how you present yourself to it that will determine your future/eventual success.

The universe is highly intelligent and speaks to you in events. You cannot change or avoid unpleasant and unhappy—and often unforeseen—situations in life, you can only change your thinking to gain control of how to move through them. Your personal problems show you exactly what you need to work on.

But there are times when there is a big glitch and the universe sends us massive events that affect everyone. When they happen, we are offered an opportunity to further the evolution of our society as a whole. Take recent events, like a global pandemic, a series of financial crises, the proliferation of misinformation, or the rise of extremism in our political system—these challenges present us with an opportunity to develop relationships with our higher forces, further our potential, and fight the war against X together.

The practice of confronting your personal X brings forward real lessons and rewards that supplement your growth. Once you gain these skills, you gain a place in the war. The way we face our personal problems and the problems in our society are precisely the same: they all boil down to how you battle your Part X.

Fighting it is the only path to true satisfaction.

Precious Time

An old James Taylor song says, "The secret of life is enjoying the passage of time." Undoubtedly true. But for most of us, time presents a huge problem. We don't have enough of it. Yet the harder we run after time, the more it recedes. A tricky substance, slipping through our fingers, taunting us. We are pressed for it. We waste it. Worst of all, we age, losing our precious store of it. Time becomes a great adversary and we can't escape the sense that we are losing the battle. We have lost the secret.

Time seems impossible to deal with because we fundamentally misunderstand its nature and its significance. Although we covet time, we treat it with little respect, as if it's an object we can buy and sell, something we can get on top of and control. The great lie of modern life is that technology makes us the masters of time. In truth, machines make time run away from us even faster. A perverse law dictates that the more machines you own, the less time you'll have. You scroll through social media feeds till midnight, the next morning you rise early to take your car to the mechanic. You get a stream of texts all day. The machines take all the time, and you have none for yourself.

Technology has caused us to forget the essential nature of time.

We have forgotten that time is sacred.

To the ancients, time was a gift of the gods, to be treated with awe and reverence. Elders were respected precisely because they had aged in the stream of time. Time was something higher than the individual, something not to be controlled but to be appreciated. In the sacred view of time, all good things come as part of a rhythmic process, whether the growth of a child or the harvesting of crops. Our culture has descended into a contempt for all things that take time. Youth is respected because it hasn't been exposed to time. Success won after long effort is less desirable than instantaneous wealth. We can't even tolerate brief periods of time when we are not being gratified, thus we eat or get high or disappear into our phones.

It is only when time is related to in a ritualized manner that it is restored to its sacred status. Rituals are the spaces in which meaning enters our lives. In the ancient world, ritual was completely bound up with time, whether through the seasons of the year or even the time of day. Ritual was the mechanism by which ancients acknowledged time as something from a higher world. They knew that if they lost their rituals, the meaning of life would fall apart. We can feel a faint echo of this in our holidays, at weddings and funerals. But what we have lost is any sense of ritual in our daily life.

We have lost our rhythm.

We don't live off the land, nor do we exist in an ancient tribal culture. This makes it harder for us to honor the inescapable rhythms of time. Until we learn how to do this, we will live in a frantic, meaningless world, trying desperately to catch up and not knowing how. There are ways to regain a proper relationship to time but, unlike the ancients, our culture and our surroundings won't help us. We must each be responsible for changing our habits. This takes great discipline, and indeed *discipline can be defined as the correct relationship to time.* The tools that can help us are submission, commitment, and patience. Used properly, they become ways of affirming time as a priceless gift. They restore the sense of ritual to modern life.

Submission has to do with your ego. The nature of the ego is that it wants to do what it wants when it wants to do it. The ego values immediate impulses far too much. There always seems to be something out there we can't afford to miss. The result is that we have great trouble concentrating on one thing for uninterrupted amounts of time. We are unable to eat a meal without watching a screen. We will interrupt an intimate conversation to answer a text. We are unable to write or study without losing our concentration or prematurely going on to something else. These activities must be treated as if there is something sacred about them. They are opportunities to restore some sense of ritual to our daily lives. If indeed they were sacred, we would not dare interrupt them—we would bring them to their proper conclusion. You must bring yourself to the point where you have no choice but to finish, regardless of how you feel at any given moment during the activity. You could say you are making the activity higher than the individual. Our whole culture rebels against this. We want to make our immediate personal impulses the highest thing. Yet true freedom comes only when we make our activities sacred in this manner.

Commitment has to do with connecting the past, present, and future. Commitment need not apply to long periods of time. In fact, it is best practiced over periods of one day or less. It implies that once you make a promise to yourself to do something, you keep that promise. If you commit to working out at ten tomorrow morning, you must show up and work out at that time. Precision counts. If you say you'll start at ten, then start at ten. You have made ten o'clock a sacred time. Not because there is anything inherently special about that time, but because the day before, you promised yourself you would do something just then. Ten o'clock becomes an opportunity to prove to yourself that you will keep your commitments. Once you get in the habit of functioning this way, life becomes a rhythm of commitment, action, commitment, action. The commitment connects you to the future when you must take the action. The action connects you to the past when you made the commitment. You will begin to experience past, present, and future as part of one continuum. It is impossible to grant time its proper respect without this sense of flowing continuity. Without it, life is a meaningless series of unconnected events. You will get to the point where you will want to keep your commitments exactly. True confidence only comes when you feel yourself function within the continuum of time.

Patience has to do with accepting the fact that things are created over time. This is based on a deeper truth, which is that we create nothing ourselves. Everything that happens in our lives, writing a book, raising a child, making a meal, building a house, depends on our participation with some larger whole. Anything we create is really a co-creation with something larger. When we were still tied to the land, this fact could never be denied. The rhythms of time were sacred back then because it was within these rhythms that the higher forces were seen to be working. Modern humanity wants to create things itself, out of its own ego. We have little interest in creating a working relationship with higher forces and thus put no value in waiting patiently for their help. The result is the tendency to despair in moments when nothing seems to be happening. The next time you find yourself in a situation that seems impossible, force yourself to note what happens in the hours and days that follow. In most cases, a solution will evolve over time. The person who has trained herself to observe this develops a faith in the creative power of time. Time is sacred precisely because it possesses this power. True confidence is impossible without the faith born of such a patient relationship to time.

Time also affects how we relate to each other. This is most evident within a family. You can define a family as a group of people who must relate to each other over time. If activities are consistently interrupted or never finished, if commitments are never kept, if no one is ever willing to wait for anything, the fabric of the family is weak. People who cannot respect time cannot respect each other. When meals or prayers become rituals, when the parents commune with each other for a short time each day, when activities are ordered in a structured and rhythmic manner, the family finds a degree of peace and coherence. As things slow down, it becomes easier for the kids to learn that they cannot get everything all at once. In turn, parents will feel less need to push their kids ahead too quickly. There is time to breathe. Higher forces can enter a family that has rhythm.

A blessing for everyone.

Positively Furious: The Positive Side of Anger

We live in an angry world. Take a drive, listen to the radio, go shopping. Chances are, you will meet at least one very angry person. Someone screams at you for making the wrong move. You're triggered—and you find yourself screaming right back. It happens so fast—as if we all have savage beasts beneath the surface waiting for a chance to emerge. And when it's over, it sticks in your mind. You mutter to yourself about the other person. Because of course it's easier to imagine how angry those around us are; it's much less pleasant to think of ourselves as angry. But that driver holding up his finger is probably more like you than you would care to admit. You've heard that the solution to the world's anger must start with you. But even that concept can make you angry.

Most angry exchanges occur on a very low level of consciousness. Emotions are felt and expressed, but few of us have any perspective about what has really happened. We have no sense of the meaning of anger in our lives. We have no guiding principles to deal with rage, no set of tools to help us see a purpose for anger. Without these, we are doomed to endlessly repeat the same experiences and walk around feeling frustrated and victimized. Anger is a strong force. Because it connects us to the most primitive parts of ourselves, we don't like to think of anger as part of our lives with a place of its own. Like all strong emotions, anger is so powerful that we cannot deal with it constructively unless we have a point of view and a preexisting plan.

First, we need to be able to find something potentially positive about anger. One striking fact is that a while after an anger incident occurs, the specific issues that provoked the anger usually seem trivial. They are almost excuses for releasing some hidden force that craves expression. This hidden force—the true nature of anger—is misunderstood in our culture. Surprisingly, this force is actually a striving for individuality. Anger is one of the initial ways that the self emerges. Think about the behavior of a two-year-old. This is the age that a child needs to start separating from his parent and start sensing his own individuality. How does he do this? With a great deal of negativity and anger. The force of these emotions helps him declare himself as separate from the parent. Anger is a first, positive step toward selfhood.

As adults, anger in its raw form is not enough to increase our feelings of individuality. We must learn to change the nature of anger for it to play a positive role in our lives. More commonly, we let it simmer inside. Many years ago, I did a single psychotherapy session with a man whom I distinctly remember as being the angriest person I had ever met. Outwardly calm, he was a barely controlled knot of envy and rage, mostly due to frustration in his writing career. Ten years later, I read a newspaper article about his death at age forty-five from widespread cancer. We can learn to transform anger into something constructive. But first, we need to understand why we hold on to anger so tightly.

Anger in adults tends to be a reaction to outer events. Details aside, the rage is a reaction to the sense that the outer world is not treating us properly. The writer I mentioned above felt the world did not appreciate his abilities as an author. But the teenager who does not like the way another kid looks at him feels just as put upon. The rage says, "The world is not fair, I'm not getting the treatment I deserve." Unconsciously, the person holds on to the rage until the world begins to treat him fairly. It lies in waiting like a coiled snake, lashing out unpredictably at the slightest provocation.

This leads us to the first principle of dealing with anger: it is inevitable. Unless you believe the world will treat you absolutely fairly every time, you will without question suffer further indignities and mistreatments. It's a part of life, unavoidable for the rest of your days. Thus, both the injury and your angry reaction are part of a natural unavoidable cycle. Once you accept this, you need not feel guilty about your reaction. On the other hand, you need not hang on to the anger since the mistreatment itself is something you have factored into your experience. The more unrealistic you are about how the world should treat you, the more shocked you will be when you are not treated well. You will take things personally every time, and not be able to let go of your anger. It's a paradox—because so many are enraged at their unjust treatment, we live in a society of walking powder kegs. We react against each other, magnifying even more the sense of unfairness each of us feels.

Those who insist the world should treat them fairly end up feeling like victims. On a national level, this has led to wars of interest groups and a splitting up of our society. The political rhetoric is itself fueled by rage. But the rage of the victim is not a constructive rage. It feeds on itself with the unconscious desire to *keep things the way they are,* so there's a reason to continue to be angry. The anger and the victimization become a form of identity that is clung to out of familiarity. In that sense, the angrier the person becomes, the less likely they are to move on with their life. Rage becomes an anchor holding them back. It's easy to think of people around you who constantly express the same kind of anger at the same situations over and over. They are stuck. The question then becomes: how can you deal with anger in a way that moves you forward in life?

It is key that anger be processed right at the moment it comes up. The longer you let it fester, the more ingrained it gets until it becomes an obstacle to healthy living. Processing anger is not the same as repressing it. Buried anger is what probably killed the writer I mentioned earlier. We need a *creative* way of working with anger so it ends up as a positive force. This involves three steps. When you find yourself enraged, take a quiet moment and focus on your anger. Block out everything else. Make the emotion as intense as possible. I call this **self-assertion**. The second step is to completely shut off the anger. This is not as difficult as it seems: Visualize yourself in a natural setting at night, looking up at the infinite number of stars. Let yourself feel inconsequential in the universe; your personal concerns will seem unimportant and you can feel your anger dissolve. This step is called **self-control**. The third step is to focus on the person who provoked your anger and send a loving energy to them. Do this intensely—do not argue with yourself about whether or not the person really deserves love. Do it as you would physical exercise, without judgment. The ability to project a loving energy to someone who has hurt you is called **active love**, and is the highest stage of selfhood. Repeat the three steps until your emotions are resolved. You have not repressed or denied your anger, you have transformed it into a different kind of energy. And each time you do this, your sense of self becomes stronger and less subject to the actions of others.

It is natural to object to this approach as passive, but this is far from the truth. Most people have no way to resolve their anger. They spend a lot of time and energy obsessing about things others have done to them and thinking of how to get that person to redress the wrong. They distract themselves and weaken their will to move forward with their lives. Their outward displays of anger may appear to be forceful and aggressive, but they actually have very little positive effect. Trapped by their own rage, they are truly the passive ones. In fact, they actually define the term "victim"—a person who is wasting his will.

Once you have learned to turn anger into love, you experience a stronger sense of self. From this new vantage point, you will be able to accept the frustrations and unfairness of life without getting tied up in knots. You will be calmer and more self-possessed. Your energies will be free to concentrate on your future. Anger no longer makes you a victim. Instead, it becomes a first step to unleashing creative forces of your higher self, forces that express themselves through love instead of hate. This higher self will give you the silent courage to move forward with your life—a courage infinitely stronger than all the screaming in the world.

Getting the Best of
Your Bad Habits

I once worked with a photographers' rep whose life was falling apart in all directions at once. Overweight, distracted, and slightly unkempt, he looked like an overgrown kid who couldn't quite remember to tuck in his shirt. You'd never guess he ran a huge agency. In truth, it ran him. He was at the beck and call of a long list of demanding artists. "I'm like a mother with thirty infants who are always hungry." Unable to say no to his clients, he'd reach the brink of exhaustion every day. He rewarded himself for his suffering with a set of personal indulgences that weakened him physically and emotionally. He'd sneak a hit of pot several times a day, never pass up a steak, and compulsively spill out a litany of his troubles to anyone within earshot, whether they wanted to hear them or not.

Business was good yet his life was a chaotic failure. He needed new offices but didn't have the energy to move. He had to get rid of several unreasonable clients but was afraid of the confrontation. Though he'd grown apart from his wife, he couldn't find the time to connect to her. As kid-like as he seemed, inside he felt old, "like I'm close to death." I told him he could regain a sense of purpose, and with it, his life force. But there was a price—he'd have to change his

bad habits. No more pot, overeating, or emotional dumping. The idea panicked him. "I can't get through the day
without that stuff. Why can't I change the other things
first?" "Because it's impossible," I answered.

His bad habits didn't just threaten his health, they
drained him of the energy he needed to move forward in his
life. The impulses for all of our bad habits travel along the
same path—a straight shot to immediate gratification
through what I call the lower channel. Whether we reach
for a cookie or a cigarette, or give vent to an outburst of
whining or rage, we are looking for an instantaneous reward. Our desires come through the lower channel in an
impulsive burst, saying *I want it now.*

Many of us do everything through the lower channel.

This man's impulse to overserve his clients was actually
a desperate attempt to win their love. Lower-channel functioning is a disaster. When the pleasure is over, we're left
with nothing. Nonetheless, most of us find it impossible to
stay out of the lower channel, even when we know the results will be harmful.

Our bad habits are driven by a demonic part of us that
wants to block our forward motion. This inner force—our
Part X—is a cunning adversary that plays tricks with our
minds. Its power comes from its ability to put us in an al-
tered state, a state where we act as if there are no consequences to our bad habits. My patient would say, "I know

the food and drugs aren't good for me, but when I indulge, the dangers don't seem real. All I can feel is my urge." When you behave as if there are no consequences, you've lost your sense of the future. Immediate pleasure is all there is. Without a future, life becomes meaningless. The genius of Part X is it makes you believe you can't function without your bad habits.

But of course you can, because you have.

Life is a struggle. It's human nature to want a reward for our pain and effort. Most of the time we are rewarded, but there is no certainty about when the reward will come or what it will be. This is the law of the universe, and it requires us to have faith in the future. But X tells us we're special, and we needn't be subject to the law. We have a right to get paid right now. In fact, X tells us that the only thing to trust is immediate gratification. Faith is unnecessary. But people without faith become weak. This man couldn't make any effort at all without the guarantee of his little rewards. He was blind to the truth. What he saw as rewards were really punishments, endangering his health and keeping him childlike. Part X had thoroughly tricked him.

Unstopped, this force turns your impulses into addictions. Every lower-channel impulse takes you outside yourself for gratification. But we are spiritual beings, and the only real satisfaction comes from connecting to higher forces. What you call these forces—God or flow or the unconscious, as I have throughout this book—doesn't matter.

These are infinite forces, found only inside ourselves. The more you go out into the material world, the further you get from these forces and the emptier you feel. To one degree or another, we all feel this inner emptiness, this hole inside. Part X lies, telling us to go outside ourselves for one more joint or piece of cake or outburst of rage—this will finally fill up the hole. Then we take ourselves even further from the inner forces that could actually satisfy the emptiness. It's an escalating cycle. The more we act out our impulse, the bigger the hole gets.

This is the essence of an addiction: *we try to fill an infinite hole with a finite experience.*

There is an old proverb that defines insanity as doing the same thing over and over hoping to get a different result.

As destructive as these patterns are, they are very hard to change. The moment we deny ourselves some gratification, we feel deprived. Part X appeals to our selfishness, telling us we should never have to feel deprived.

The only way to fight this is to have an equally selfish reason not to give in to our impulses. In other words, we need to find a reward in depriving ourselves. In the lower-channel, purely material world, this seems impossible. But when you see life in terms of energies instead of just things, it all changes. And it changes fast.

Each time you restrain your impulses, you close off the lower channel. A dynamic inversion occurs—when you curb the impulse you invert its energy, holding it inside yourself. This energy gets transformed and then emerges in a more powerful form through the higher channel. This path has the power to create. The higher channel connects you to the world of flow with its infinite forces. When you function out of the higher channel, higher forces help you move toward your goals.

This powerful energy is the reward you get when you deprive yourself of an addiction. And in this higher channel, the energy accrues. Every act of restraint puts more in the piggy bank. You are making an investment in yourself. The energy of the higher channel gives you courage, creativity, and a sense of purpose.

This dynamic inversion of energy isn't just a concept, it's a tool you can use whenever you have a destructive impulse. Let's say you are craving a candy bar. The anticipated pleasure is what opens up the lower channel. I've found that the best way to close it back down is to feel the pain instead, probably because lower-channel addictions always lead to pain eventually. The moment you feel the sugar craving, connect to that sense of pain. The more you practice, the better you'll get. Feel the pain literally closing down the channel. Then silently call for help. Do this as passionately as possible. Imagine that a host of spiritual guides descend to lift you out of the lower channel. I see them in white robes; you can use any image that works. If the concept of guides bothers you, think of them as pure forces from out of your own unconscious. Finally, imagine yourself walking out into the world with these guiding figures. Your purpose is to be of service to the world. Again, teach yourself to quickly create this feeling of being of service. Service is the most direct way to open the higher channel. You'll literally feel your impulse for sugar dissolve.

We are an addicted society. Immediate gratification is our religion. Talking about self-control is weak. The only way to really help ourselves is to change our own habits. This sets a force in motion that can change our future.

Decisions, Decisions

No character sticks in my mind more than Hamlet. This is not due simply to Shakespeare's brilliance. There is something fascinating about the dilemma of someone unable to make a decision. Four hundred years later, the tortured spirit of the Prince of Denmark lives in us all. In fact, it is fair to say that indecisiveness is one of the salient features of the modern soul. Stripped of the certainties of tradition, separated from the support of church, family, and community, we are increasingly left on our own to decide our fate. In one sense we have a degree of freedom inconceivable to prior generations. But along with that come levels of anxiety our ancestors could never have imagined. We have so many choices but we can't seem to make the smallest one. What is it about the modern condition that makes us so indecisive?

Shakespeare's play gives us a clue. Hamlet was written at the turn of the seventeenth century, coinciding with the birth of the modern world. The new emphasis on reason and logic led to a scientific view of the universe, and eventually to the industrial revolution. This new approach had profound psychological effects. On the positive side, the ability to reason affords us a high degree of individuality and sense of freedom; indeed these qualities are the hallmark of the modern person. But thinking can never bring certainty, and, since it can cut you off from your instincts, actually increases uncertainty. Even theoretical physics admits that the rational observer can never predict what will happen (the Heisenberg Uncertainty Principle). In one sense, Hamlet was ahead of his time. His raging indecisiveness and self-doubt mark him as the prototype for modern humanity. His ability to think and reason isolated him from the world and paralyzed his ability to act. This is why he fascinates us so; his dilemma is our dilemma.

The problem with reasoning is that it suggests you can get something absolutely right. However, this is true only if you could know every single relevant fact about the issue at hand. Unfortunately, life doesn't work that way. If you are deciding to start a new business, you cannot possibly know what will happen to the economy in eighteen months. If you are deciding to send your child to camp, you can't possibly know what the personalities of the other children in her bunk will be. Even if you are deciding something as simple as to go to a movie, you cannot know how crowded it will be or what the traffic will be like. We live in an unpredictable and constantly changing universe that cannot be known in any complete or absolute sense. Thus, the notion that you can rationally make decisions based on logically analyzing all the factors does not apply to real life. Abraham Lincoln, the most famous decision-maker in history, said that he never had all the facts he needed when he made big decisions. Eisenhower, after ordering the invasion of Normandy, was so unsure of his decision that he withdrew, ill, to his room, and slept for the rest of the day.

The belief that you can think your way through to the "right" decision creates a false sense of comfort. You mistakenly believe you have grasped and analyzed every aspect of the situation. This would only be possible in a world that has stopped moving. But there is a strong attraction to this illusion. If indeed we could live in a completely knowable, static world, then once we decided something it would be decided for all time. *No further decisions would be necessary.* That would be nice, but it's not possible. Most bad decision-making is driven by this impossible dream. We want to get our decisions "right" and then hope that the world will stop changing, that we will never face uncertainty again. The result is that even small decisions take on a life-or-death weight. We feel that if we make a good decision we are saved and that if we make a bad decision we are ruined. In truth, good decision or not, life will go on. Besides death and taxes, the one sure thing about life is that it will demand that you make further decisions, often in the same areas you have struggled with in the past. You may agonize over what school your child should attend, finally make a choice, and pray that she gets in, which she does, only to find she hates it and wants out after the first year.

A new decision approaches. Because a new decision always approaches.

Once you let go of the magical belief that you can get

things right, you are ready to look at decisions as part of a process. You no longer believe that you can make such a good decision that you will be excused from further uncertainty and further decisions. Each decision becomes just one step in a process of decision-making that goes on for the rest of your life. With very few exceptions, no one decision will save you or destroy you (although it may seem so at the time). But what *will* change your life and relieve you of tremendous pressure and self-doubt is to learn and apply the rules of correct decision-making. First, you must move your focus away from the *results* of your decisions and instead toward *how* you make the decisions. If you make them properly, even if the outcome is not good, you will strengthen yourself in these areas:

Tolerating Loss

It is human nature to try to avoid loss when making decisions. The illusion that we can be right brings with it the desire to believe that the city in which we live, the career path we follow, the politician we support, is the best choice. We disparage the path not taken because doing so protects us against the sense that, given the choice we made, we were forced to lose something. But in fact, loss is inherent in all decisions. Decisions are limiting by nature. If I live in Florida, I lose the ability to live in Colorado. If I become a teacher, I lose the opportunity to be an engineer. If I go to a certain movie, I miss the other movie playing the same night. As obvious as this seems, we forget it all the time. In one sense, every decision you make limits the world you live in. This is unavoidable. Fortunately, it is this sense of outer limitation that makes us stronger spiritually. Once we accept the inherently limited nature of the outer world, our inner world opens up and we are forced to look inside ourselves for fulfillment. Decisions can become tools for spiritual growth. And paradoxically, this inner-directed mode of decision-making actually creates better external results in the long run.

But even if a decision does not turn out well, it does not mean you are a failure as a decision-maker. Good decision-makers expect losses. Not only do they recover from them well, they anticipate that they will have to tolerate further losses in the future. Freed from the need to be "right," they have less fear and less paralysis.

Clarifying Your Values

Proper decision-making forces you to clarify what you value. There will always be an information gap, and it is precisely in that uncertain place that you will have to commit. Thus the time-honored practice of making a list of the pros and cons can never be adequate. There will always be pros and cons of which you are unaware. Instead, you can define what your *highest value* is in a given situation. This does not necessarily imply a moral value. Ask yourself what is important above all else to you. You may choose to live in

Minnesota, despite the weather, because being near family is your highest value. You may choose to become a pediatrician, despite the difficult working conditions, because service to children is your highest value. The factor that is most important to you becomes the transcendent variable in the decision, large or small. And when you consider your decisions with hindsight and feel that you made a mistake, you will be able to see the loss as worthwhile because you were guided by what you valued most. You will make plenty of mistakes, we all do, but you will become increasingly able to define what is most important to you. Nothing could be more valuable.

Trusting Your Instincts

Instincts are a form of intelligence different from reason. They come to us all at once and demand to be expressed in action. You cannot tap into your instincts unless you have some relationship to your unconscious. Two keys to connecting to the unconscious are to rely on mind pictures instead of words, and to use your sleep time as a doorway to higher information. When you face a decision, try this: Before going to sleep, pick one possible course of action and create images of what you see happening if you were to go in that direction. Then switch to an opposing course of action and again create images of what might happen. Erase both sets of pictures and go to sleep. Be very alert when you wake up. You may have a strong instinct to go one way or the other. For big decisions, you may have to repeat this technique many times. Franklin Delano Roosevelt was famous for taking short naps before he made decisions. Since this is a nonlogical technique that is, in effect, asking for help from forces that transcend the conscious mind, it may seem strange at first. But the more you observe your own decisions and those of others, the more you'll realize how small a role logic plays in what we end up doing. If you are afraid to act on your instincts, you will lose touch with them. Paralyzed, you may become like Hamlet, and turn your life into a tragedy.

The Only True Success

"Let me tell you about the very rich," said F. Scott Fitzgerald. "They are different from you and me." They fly in their Gulfstream jets, build huge homes, and have every earthly need taken care of by a legion of staff. They seem to reside in a universe with its own rules, exempt from the forces that dominate the lives of the rest of us. Once I started working with the super-rich on a daily basis, I discovered that Mr. Fitzgerald was dead wrong. Money does protect the rich from most of life's physical discomforts (except illness, of course), but emotionally and spiritually, the rich inhabit the same world as the rest of us. They are subject to the same challenges and pitfalls. Yet we want to believe that the rich are different because it reinforces our belief in the magical power of money. If money truly is the bottom line of human achievement, then the rich had better be different. Otherwise, what would be the point of our society's insane fixation on wealth?

Greed alone can't explain this obsession. How we feel and act are determined by what we think is real. Our culture tells us daily that money is the bottom line of reality, the ultimate value in the universe. This idea is not as crazy as it sounds. Money does have a quality that coincides with the underlying nature of the universe. Each time there is a financial transaction, goods and services change hands and there is movement, there is *flow*. Think of flow as the dynamic force that drives *everything*. The very core of the universe is alive, ceaselessly creating new things. It is human nature to crave this ultimate reality. But money has become a substitute for this moving force, causing us to misunderstand the meaning of success. And using money as a model of success is ripping our society apart.

The truest model of success is right in front of us. The universe itself is remarkably successful. Why? Because it has created endless life in an unbroken stream for tens of thousands of years. Each of us is a tiny model of the universe and we have within us this same need to ceaselessly create. It is only in the activity of creating that we feel truly successful and alive. No amount of money can replace that feeling. I learned this lesson while treating a man who had amassed a personal fortune of over a billion dollars by buying and selling companies with his younger partner. When the partnership ended, my patient became severely depressed, lacking the confidence to create new business opportunities on his own. I can still hear his words: "If I can't create new money then I'm no longer successful." This statement reveals elements of greed and neurosis, but it also contains a profound truth. All of us need to feel able to create some sense of newness in our lives. We need to feel ourselves in flow every day. Unfortunately, this man couldn't equate newness with anything but new money, a failing that almost destroyed him.

Real success is the aliveness you feel when you create something new. It has nothing to do with external results. Success occurs when you inhabit a space in the universe where you connect with flow. Once you learn how to find this success universe, you will feel that the future is full of endless possibility. Its opposite is the failure universe, a limited world where nothing new is being created. There you feel burdened and victimized, unable to foresee a positive future. Every day becomes a success or failure depending on which world you choose to live in. This changes the whole game. A life well lived is one where you find your way into the success universe and stay there.

This is not an intellectual construct; when you enter this world of flow you will actually feel totally different.

How do you find your way to this creative state? Follow the model of the universe and its cycle of creation. Observe the great cycles of evolution. Genetic mutation is the equivalent of the human instinct to make a change. The universe takes action in the form of creating a new organism. The consequence is whether or not the new form survives. Look at the profound success that resulted from this cycle—the human race itself. And the cycle is ceaseless. Each consequence leads to a new instinct, which starts the cycle again. Instinct, action, consequence, instinct, action, consequence—the universe never quits. The truly successful person has the courage to work this cycle over and over again. Most people are not willing to do this; they step out of the cycle and lose touch with the success universe and its sense of possibilities. That is why most people feel like failures. Instead, imitate this creative action cycle and apply it to your own life in the following ways.

Listen to Your Instincts

As I said in the previous essay, an instinct is a form of intelligence that does not come in words and that wants to be expressed through action. Instincts don't come with the clarity that thoughts do. Their "rightness" can't be proved logically. An instinct is right to the extent it feels connected to who you are. Because most of us aren't used to living by our instincts, we don't trust them. There is only one way to clearly know your instincts. *You must exercise them.* If you have the sense that you could write screenplays but have never tried, you must evoke the creative action cycle to find out. This means writing a script and suffering the consequences. Of course, everyone is worried about the failure that will prove their instinct was "wrong." *The secret is that it doesn't matter if you were wrong.* The only thing that matters is that you train yourself to follow your instincts over and over. Each time you do, you activate the magic of creation and even if it doesn't work out, your confidence in your instincts will increase. And that confidence is success.

Take Action

Unlike intellectual concepts, instinctual intelligence has no value until you act on it. Most of us have tremendous problems taking action. We passively wait, hoping to get into a state of mind where we will be more motivated, less afraid. This reflects a complete misunderstanding of success. We need to take action regardless of how we feel. Why? Because we are not taking action to win or achieve some specific result. We are taking action because it is action itself that will change our state. When you have an instinct, you must train yourself to act on it immediately. This activates the cycle and puts you in touch with the creative forces of the universe. These forces will change your state at the very moment you take the action. Whether you succeed or fail is irrelevant.

Accept the Consequences

Just as most of us misunderstand the role of action, we also misunderstand the meaning of consequences. Consequences are not always good. Your first screenplay doesn't sell. Your start-up company goes bankrupt. It is natural to allow a negative consequence to reflect back on yourself and mean you are a failure. But in our new view, you are a failure only if you step off the cycle of creation. To someone committed to the cycle, a negative consequence merely represents a correction. Remember: whatever you are creating, you are not creating alone. Everything new is a coproduction between you and the life forces of the universe. A correction means you approached these higher forces in the wrong way. You may discover you are a novelist, not a screenwriter, or that you need to start a different kind of business. Co-creating with higher forces is a profound activity and we rarely get it right on the first pass, or even the first hundred passes. Once you accept this you begin to feel a divine wisdom from even the most negative consequences. At this point you can't be stopped. You can create every day for the rest of your life.

And that feels better than all the money in the world.

Loving the One You're With

Our culture is marked by the relentless pursuit of the better deal. We take it as our divine right to go for the bigger house, the faster car, the more prestigious job. Driven by a blind force, we look outside ourselves for more. The result is a frenzy of activity, powered by the fear of missing something, which exhausts us emotionally and leaves us spiritually empty. Nowhere is this pursuit more destructive than in our intimate relationships. Wanting a better car is one thing; wanting a better wife or husband is quite another. We have brought an acquisitive, judgmental force into a place where it does not belong—the realm of love.

I witnessed an extreme form of this in a patient of mine, an actor in his midthirties, happily married with two children, who had struggled for years in his career. Out of the blue, he got the lead in a film that became a hit. Suddenly he was a movie star, an event for which he was emotionally unprepared. It was understandable that he would immediately trade up to a better home and buy some new toys. But that was not enough. He began to talk to me about "getting a better wife." As twisted as it sounds, he felt his newfound success entitled him to something more in the marriage department, and he was driven to find it before his career took a downturn and he lost his window of opportunity.

The most shocking part was his fantasy about what the new woman should be like. She would have to be rich and famous on her own, incredibly charismatic, with a jet-set lifestyle. He was quick to admit that his present wife was beautiful, loving, and quite creative in her own right. But her human qualities paled in comparison to this fantasy companion. He searched for his ideal among the famous actresses his new status allowed him to meet. Each seemed promising from afar, but inevitably he would find enough flaws to convince him that she wasn't it. During his hunt, his wife filed for divorce and within months, he was begging her to take him back. She did, and only then did he begin to understand what was involved in a mature relationship.

This man almost destroyed his marriage in the search for an illusion. The specific attributes he was seeking weren't important. *What he was really looking for was someone with the magical ability to change the nature of reality.* Reality is uncertain, often painful, and makes constant demands of us. Reality requires work. The consumer culture is continuously selling us on the magic of products we acquire, so why not go for some real magic—a person who could exonerate us from reality itself. Such a person could lead us into an alternate universe where we feel good all the time, where life is easy. Problem is, no human being, no matter how attractive, has this power. All we can do is *project* this ability onto another flawed human being. But once we spend time with them, we always end up disappointed. They seem no more magical than we are. How does this happen?

Think of a movie projector showing a film. The screen must be at a distance from the projector; if it's too close, no image will appear. The same is true with people. It is only possible to project magical properties onto a person if they are at a distance. As you get to know them, the emotional distance disappears and with it goes the image. You see them as they really are, and it's a huge disappointment. So, you project onto yet another person, the more unavailable the better—one who's married to someone else, or uninterested in you, or one you haven't even met—to keep the distance and keep your dream alive.

Eventually, it dawns on most people that this supreme class of superior partners doesn't exist. At that point, they become more willing to work with the person they're with and to understand the reality of love.

To put it simply, love is a process. All processes require endless work because perfection is never achieved. Accepting this fact is not thrilling, but it is the first step to happiness. You can work on finding satisfaction in your relationship the same way you'd work on your piano playing or your garden.

This takes some inspiration—you need to feel that the work is actually good for you and believe that you have a reasonable chance of succeeding (even though doing the work is itself the success). Otherwise, you will quit the process and go back to looking outside your relationship for the magical high only an unknown at a distance can give. Here are the areas to work on and some effective tools:

Fantasy Control

It's human nature to fantasize about other partners. We tell ourselves that merely fantasizing is a free and harmless pleasure, and often it is. But beyond a certain point, fantasizing becomes an obstacle to a relationship. You will know that your fantasies are out of control if they are long and involved, if you use them as an antidote to dissatisfaction with your partner, and if they bear no relationship whatsoever to reality. Fantasies are constructed of images and therefore hold a tremendous amount of emotional energy (that's why we love the movies). The more energy you pour into your magical non-partner and fantasy life, the less energy you will have for your real partner and your real life. Be honest about the amount of time you spend in the clouds. If you are out of control in this area, which is very common, you must develop the will to interrupt each fantasy. This includes sexual fantasies, the most compelling kind. You'll resent this at first, but each time you come down to earth you're telling yourself that you are a committed adult who is strong enough to face reality. This will make you more satisfied with yourself, a precondition to becoming satisfied with any partner.

Judgment

It's hard enough to accept that our fantasies have huge power. It's even harder to accept the power that our judgments have. When you think about some unavailable person, it's easy to be filled with positive thoughts about their intelligence, personality, sexuality, etc. The truth is, these thoughts are nothing more than judgments based on emotion, and they often turn out to be false. Most of our reactions to even our own partners have less to do with objective truth than with our *thoughts* about who he or she is. It is insulting to our egos to accept that most of our judgments are subjective and not inherently "right." But if you admit this, you become free to select thoughts that enhance your relationship. First, you have to gain control over negative judgments about your partner. As their failings become obvious in the course of a relationship, we all tend to have more and more negative thoughts. We fixate on their weaknesses. But our negative judgments are not right, they are a product of the disappointment that our partner is not perfect. The process of loving requires that you catch yourself having these negative thoughts and dissolve them from your mind, replacing them with positive ones. You must actively construct thoughts about their good attributes, and let these thoughts renew feelings of attraction toward them. All this effort pays off; not only will you feel more content with your partner, but this new mental self-control carries an inherent power that will make you more confident and emotionally stable for the rest of your life.

Emotional Expression

We like to believe that the emotions we express to our partners are based on how we really feel about them. But it is also true that the emotions we express *determine* how we feel about them. Try this: Whenever you are with your partner, particularly when you're alone, talk to them and touch them as if they are tremendously desirable. Do this with more passion than you may feel. Try this consistently for a week. I guarantee your partner will become more attractive to you. Once you see how effective it is to express positive emotions regularly, you will accept it as part of the work that is required in the process of loving. Your partner will experience the effort you've made and will usually reciprocate. Not only will you make your relationship better, but you'll learn how to inspire others through the power of your own emotional self-expression.

We have not been trained to think of love as requiring a tremendous amount of disciplined effort. But like it or not, it's the reality of love. Once you set about the work, you will feel forward movement in your relationship and have hope about its future. Eventually, you will see a higher purpose in your relationship. This is your opportunity to accept and practice the endless work that love demands. And there's no greater teacher than the work of love.

Standing Alone

As a kid on the streets of New York, I was constantly afraid of being beaten up. The first sting of a punch would send tears to my eyes. I became adept at avoiding fights. Years later I studied the martial arts. As part of the training we were forced to spar with one another. To my surprise I discovered I could take a tremendous blow with very little effect. Why did a punch thrown in anger hurt me so much more than one thrown in karate class? The answer was that there was an *emotional* pain affiliated with getting hit in a fight that was not present in a sparring session. It is the pain that comes with the shocking realization that someone else actually *wants to hurt you*. The most extreme form of this occurs in soldiers in battle for the first time. When bullets start to fly, their first reaction, even before fear, is shock. They cannot believe someone would want to kill them. Wars, or even a fistfight, are extreme forms of human conflict. But our reactions to them reveal an illusion most of us share that severely limits our ability to live life to the fullest.

We like to believe it is possible to avoid conflict. This includes not just extreme forms of physical conflict, but the more common forms in which we are verbally and emotionally attacked. How is it possible to maintain such an illusion when we see so much conflict around us? We are quite willing to accept that *others* will be attacked. But deep in our hearts each of us believes we have some special goodness that protects us. We are shocked when someone attacks us. We say to ourselves, "I am a good person, how could someone want to hurt me?" This is the reaction of a child, not an adult. Children want to be secure in the adoration of their parents and those around them. As long as they feel loved they believe themselves to be in a safe universe, a world without hostility. Growing up is precisely the process of leaving such a protected world and entering a reality where you are subject to the attacks of others, often undeserved.

The most painful attack one can experience is to be misunderstood or even hated. If the child inside us wants to be validated and adored, then this is the exact opposite experience. You ask a neighbor to turn down his stereo at midnight and he accuses you of being a nosy jerk. You get up to give a speech and get shouted down by a loudmouthed heckler. You present a new idea at a work meeting and are rudely insulted by your boss. Hatred and misunderstanding imply not just that someone doesn't like you, but that they fundamentally misinterpret who you are. The world fails to see that you have good intentions. Since the child part of us is so identified with our goodness, it feels like character assassination.

We are becoming a society in which no one will take a stand. Social media culture has intensified the fear of hatred and misunderstanding since the backlash comes faster than ever before. It has made our leaders overly desirous of the validation of the electorate to the point where they are usually afraid to take a clear position. Using polls to tell us what we want to hear hardly qualifies as leadership. The media is also capable of creating a frenzy that can destroy the guilty and the innocent alike.

Each of us must learn to take a stand in our own lives. To do this, you must be confident that you can endure the hatred and misunderstanding that will inevitably come your way. Most of us take attacks very personally. We get caught up in the "unfairness" of it all. This only makes the pain worse. Instead, we can find a higher meaning in the pain and learn to see hatred and misunderstanding as an *opportunity to find our true individuality*. The childish part of you that needs approval is not your real self. It is only when this part of you is *not* getting the adoration it craves that you can discover another, deeper part of yourself, one that does not live as a reflected image in the minds of others. Without conflict, no one would ever discover this deeper self. Experiences of hatred and misunderstanding shatter our egos so we can discover who we really are.

Only when you find this independent self are you truly adult. In our culture we have confused *physical* adulthood with an authentic spiritual adulthood. The ancient world understood the difference much better than we do. Teenagers were initiated into adulthood by the tribe through sacred rituals that encouraged them to give up their childish needs for safety and come into their adult powers. A person was not allowed to sit in a tribal council until the age of sixty, since it was assumed that only those who had reached this advanced age had purged themselves of their immature needs for validation from the outside world. Older adults were respected precisely *because* they were more removed from the world and thus had the wisdom of real selfhood.

The modern person is initiated into adulthood by *life itself*, particularly by experiences of hatred and misunderstanding. Attacks do not mean you have done something wrong, rather they are tests of your spiritual adulthood. A businessman who was my patient exemplifies this modern form of initiation. He was a brilliant, ambitious forty-year-old who developed an innovative high-tech product. When the product hit the market, another company publicly accused him of stealing the idea from them. They sued, and he received a great deal of negative publicity. Not only were the charges unjust, but because he prided himself on his originality and integrity, his ego was crushed. Publicly humiliated, he withdrew from the business world for two years fearing his career was over. To his surprise, he found he was able to live without his former fame and position. A year later he introduced another unique product that brought him money and recognition beyond his wildest dreams. He built a huge company and became known as a fair, levelheaded leader. He considered himself blessed to have had the initial experience of hatred and misunderstanding, no matter how painful it had been. Without it, he was certain the success would have gone to his head, making him an erratic leader and ultimately an unhappy person. He wielded his new power well because he knew he could walk away from it.

For most of us, it is a series of small, day-to-day experiences of hatred and misunderstanding that offer the opportunity to gain our adult selves. I worked with a young mother raising her first child, a bright and willful five-year-old girl. The mother was insecure, needing her daughter's constant adoration and approval. When the mother tried to set boundaries, she found it almost intolerable to stand up to her daughter's accusations of "you don't love me." The result was a role reversal in which the mother was afraid to set limits of any kind for her daughter, particularly around bedtime. The more the child got her way, the more irritable and hyperactive she became. It was not until the mother realized that it was her *responsibility* to bear the hatred and misunderstanding of her daughter that she could regain the parental role. Until this was accomplished, the child did not have a mother. This problem is so common today that every parent needs to make a point of supporting each other in taking unpopular stands with their own children. Without this, there can be no order in a family. Children who receive no opposition when young will not be able to tolerate any opposition once grown. They will never spiritually grow up.

Once you train yourself to see the opportunity in hatred and misunderstanding, you will receive the benefits of real individuality. You will be able to form your own opinions regardless of the popular view. You will be able to express your own ideas and hold on to them even under attack. With this new strength, you become a natural leader.

This is spiritual adulthood.

And it is infinitely more satisfying than all the adoration in the world.

Faith: No Doubt About It

Decades ago, I was on my usual route to the dry cleaner's. As I walked up the block, I came upon a long line of people of all ages and descriptions. They moved at a snail's pace but no one complained. Far ahead I saw the line snake through lights and cameras at the entrance to an office building. This being Los Angeles, I assumed a movie was being filmed and the crowd was queued up for the opportunity to be cast as extras. Why else were they waiting so patiently under the fierce late-summer sun? But then, as I got closer to the entrance, I saw men and women bending down and placing bouquets onto the largest pile of flowers I had ever seen. Media people were everywhere. I asked one of them what was going on. She looked at me like I was crazy and said gravely, "This is the British consulate." Only then did I link this street ceremony with Princess Diana's death the week before. The purposeful, solemn faces of the crowd suddenly made sense. The mourners were waiting in the hundred-degree heat for the opportunity to participate in something bigger and more meaningful than the ordinary experience of their day-to-day lives. For them it was a spiritual experience.

There was no question that Princess Diana used her celebrity to call attention to important issues. But it does not downgrade her life to ask why she was of such transcendent importance to these everyday Americans. They had no personal or even national connection to her. Yet on some level she answered a deep yearning in each of them. Like all of us, they craved a connection with some higher force. And as is typical in our society, they sought this higher force in the outer world. Diana's superficial attributes of youth, position, and glamour made her an obvious choice for their projections. This reveals a tragedy larger than her untimely death. To the extent we make people and things in the outer world our ultimate sources of meaning, we fail ourselves. The key challenge we face is to create an inner experience of something higher. Whether you call this God, or flow, or a higher power doesn't matter. What does matter is that you do the work to find this force inside yourself. Only then have you found your true individuality.

Most of us cannot make the jump into the inner world. We lack faith. Faith is the force that gives us peace and certainty regardless of our outer circumstances. In the long run, life is intolerable without faith. Its lack tends to be most evident to us over the holidays, which is why the end of the year is such an empty time for many of us. The glut of gifts and parties mocks this inner void. But the break in the normal course of events that the holidays afford can be an opportunity to make a conscious decision to develop faith. And indeed you can systematically develop a sense of faith, just as you can develop your muscles in a gym. But in order to do so you must give up your fixation on the outer world.

Faith is a deeply held conviction that there is a higher meaning in life that cannot be proved by outer events. Our modern minds rebel against this. What we believe, we believe because we have evidence that "proves" its truth. This works well in science but not in human affairs. The past century, the century of science, has been the scene of carnage and suffering on a scale never before seen in human history. Demanding proof of issues of faith is like using a screwdriver to bang in a nail. It is the wrong approach. Think about what a scientist does. His basic attitude is to believe nothing until it can be proved. Only if there is outer proof does he accept any piece of information as true. Thus, the scientist always starts from the position of doubt. You could say he operates within a doubt system. We have misapplied this scientific attitude to spiritual issues: We demand proof of higher, inner forces. But in doing so, we activate our own doubt system, putting ourselves in an inner state where faith is impossible. The result is the mass neurosis and insecurity we see around us.

The human dilemma is that the important things in life are unprovable. It is precisely because faith does not require proof that it has so much power. You cannot prove that you love your parent, for example. Yet you know you do. It has nothing to do with logic or the intellect. Faith, too, is a different kind of knowledge. You could call it living knowledge because it only exists to the extent it lives inside you as an experience. This is not the type of knowledge you acquire once and for all. Living knowledge, like living things, requires constant effort to keep it alive. In order to have the peace of mind and confidence that faith provides, you must learn the practice of faith. This practice is a way of life that develops a spiritual organ—your higher self. It is the part of us capable of experiencing forces much larger than ourselves. And it experiences these forces with absolute certainty. But the higher self is like a musical instrument: If you don't practice regularly, it is useless. Daily living presents us with three opportunities to build up this alive knowledge.

Renouncing Immediate Gratification

One of the reasons we have trouble resisting the extra piece of cake or the third drink is that we don't connect it with anything higher than the immediate situation. You don't want to gain the extra pounds but that tends to be a weak motivation in the face of the intense pleasure staring you in the face. The only way to effectively motivate yourself to renounce pleasure is to feel that in the very act of renouncing it, you are building up a higher force inside. It's as if you deposit a penny in a spiritual piggy bank right at that moment. If you do this regularly, the deposits add up to a sense of spiritual power. You will begin to feel control over yourself and mastery of the physical world around you. You learn to see the renouncing of immediate gratification as getting something rather than giving something up.

Underlying this approach to self-discipline is the idea that everything is interconnected. Every action we take, every situation in which we find ourselves, is part of one unity. Resisting the urge to scream at your spouse, controlling your appetite, or not giving in to laziness are all related. If you practice this you will feel the connection. This sense that everything matters changes your view of the world around you. Your life will no longer seem like a chaotic series of disconnected events.

Trusting Process

The important things in life can be achieved only as part of a process. Starting a new business, writing a book, or loving your spouse all require an infinite number of small steps. We all have trouble participating in process because at the moment we take any one step, we have no guarantee it will result in success. There is always a point when we resent the effort we have to make and want to quit. Paradoxically, these dark moments are what give us the opportunity to develop faith. If during these times of demoralization when the outer world promises nothing you find the will to push yourself forward, you are relying on higher, inner forces. That is faith. As I've said, the higher self doesn't care about results. To exist it needs to participate in ceaseless process.

Finding Meaning in Events

As camp doctor during his internment at Auschwitz, psychiatrist Viktor Frankl made a careful study of which prisoners lived and which died. He came to the conclusion that faith was the force that gave the survivors the strength to endure unimaginable hardships. He found that the prisoners with the most faith were the ones who could find meaning in even the harshest events of fate. He defined meaning as a unique demand upon the individual from the future. With this view, each event in your life, no matter how difficult, becomes a specific and personal demand upon you to develop certain strengths. It takes great effort, but if you see it as your spiritual responsibility to find a higher meaning in events, you will predictably feel a greater degree of faith.

I can offer no outer proof that these exercises work to build faith. But there is inner proof. The proof is that you will change as a human being and feel more alive.

A Model Relationship

Romeo and Juliet is perhaps the most lyrical and romantic of Shakespeare's works. But beyond its beauty lies a warning. A purely romantic model of a relationship ends in tragedy. We've all had the experience of selecting a partner based on passion, only to see the excitement fade until nothing was left.

Our culture is the most naïvely romantic in the world. We are led to believe that love will conquer all, especially if you marry the quarterback or the homecoming queen. But our extraordinarily high rate of divorce attests to the fact that strong emotion is not enough when it comes to selecting a mate. Romance and passion are irrational and unpredictable forces. Therefore they should not be the criteria for judging the suitability of a new person or the value of an ongoing relationship. Precisely because relationships are so emotional, we need a dispassionate, objective way to evaluate them. If you have a model for what every relationship must be, regardless of who the partner is, then you can have an idea of what is fair to expect. A model can help you see where you need to heal problems in a relationship, or can give you the clarity to leave a person who is not good for you.

Before you can recognize a healthy relationship, you must understand the nature of a bad relationship, which I spoke about earlier but will revisit here. Like an invisible magnet, there is a force that draws us to people who are not good for us. Put simply, this force is the belief in magic. We want to find in the other person the superhuman ability to change the nature of our lives. But no other person can exempt us from reality: life is uncertain, often painful, and most of all an endless process requiring work. Nonetheless, it is human nature to cling to the illusion that we can live in an alternate reality where life is easy. We want our partner to magically take us to this other world. We project a glowing power onto them because it is what we want to see. Blinded by our own fantasy, it becomes easy to get involved with the wrong person. Inevitably we become disillusioned. Nothing has changed. But false hope springs eternal. We keep trying to resurrect our original high. Maybe things will return to the way they were at the beginning. To leave means not only being alone, but shattering the dream of being excused from life's difficulties. Paralyzed, we stay around too long. Only when you realize that nobody can exempt you from the pain and effort of living will you stop looking for magic in your relationships. At that point a whole universe of immature people stops looking attractive.

Good relationships are based on a higher bond. This bond is not something that automatically comes with the right partner, no matter how many great qualities he or she has. Rather, it is a separate entity bigger than either of the individuals involved. It is a way of making the connection between them sacred. No other factor—whether it be career demands, another person, or even the moods of one of the partners—will be allowed to break that commitment. A higher bond is a living thing that must be tended every day. The moment you stop working on it, the higher bond begins to fall apart. But it's well worth the effort to keep it alive. When two people place the bond above their own immediate needs and insecurities, they have created something that will give them energy and inspiration even in the darkest of circumstances. The higher bond is only as strong as the work it takes to sustain it. In a sense, you could say that the bond is actually made out of work. Immature relationships are the opposite. They are made out of the hope for magic, the weakest of ingredients. The higher bond doesn't exclude romance and passion, it transcends them.

Once you make the higher bond the foundation for your relationships, you have a realistic model for evaluating your partner or potential partner. You must make the commitment to work with a partner on this bond, and in turn, the key question becomes "Are they a person who will work with me on creating this bond?" If they are not, then it doesn't matter how fast they make your heart flutter. Eventually you will be miserable. There are three basic qualities a partner must have in order to build the bond: initiative, sacrifice, and empathy. They need not score an A in all three (nor do you), but they must at least make a consistent effort in each area. Once you learn to focus on these qualities, you have an objective and constant set of parameters with which to judge a spouse or lover. You need no longer be blinded by your emotions.

Initiative

Someone who is passive cannot contribute to forming a higher bond. In a relationship, each party has the responsibility for consistently reaching out to the other person. This includes taking it upon themselves to help their partner before they are asked. It includes initiating communication with the other person on a daily basis. It includes planning mutual activities. In general, if your partner has initiative, you will feel an energy coming toward you from them. If you sense that you never get anything from the other person without having to ask for it, then they lack initiative. Codependent personalities fool themselves into thinking that a bond can exist based solely on their giving emotionally to their partners. This is impossible. The bond must go both ways. Likewise, I have had patients tell themselves they are in a romantic relationship with a person despite the fact that that person rarely calls and never takes the initiative to plan anything. They are wasting their time. On the other hand, you have a good partner if you sense that they make a willful effort to connect to you at those times when they are tired, distracted, or self-absorbed. This sort of commitment is based on goodwill and maturity, and is thus long-lasting.

Sacrifice

Building the higher bond requires us to sacrifice our own personal pleasures and purposes, at least to a degree. Immature individuals want to be in relationships without giving up anything. Because they live in an unreal world, they pretend they can enjoy the benefits of a relationship without paying a price. The higher bond is a spiritual force, and spiritual forces can't be built up without the sacrifice of some lower desire. For those who can feel its power, the higher bond will naturally inspire them to make sacrifices. A good partner realizes that when they give up an activity for the sake of the relationship (watching sports events is a classic I have seen in my practice throughout the years), they are strengthening the higher bond right at that moment. They see the value and make the sacrifice quickly and without complaint. Beware of a partner who has no capacity for sacrifice.

Empathy

This means your partner should be emotionally sensitive to you. For the most part, they should be in touch with what you are feeling. This does not mean they should be a mind reader or focused on your emotions every moment. But if you consistently feel they are out of touch with you, don't know what mood you are in, and, particularly, don't know how you are feeling toward them, they have poor empathy. From my experience, I have no question that women as a group are better at this than men, but it is fair to expect a man to work on this skill. I have seen even the most brusque and aggressive males improve greatly once they became afraid they would lose their spouse if they remained out of touch. It is common for the spouse with poor empathy to accuse their partner of being too demanding when the partner complains. Do not accept this. Without the depth of an empathic connection, worked on daily, there can be no higher bond.

Relationships engender the deepest emotions human beings can feel. As a result, our ability to judge them is often distorted. The beauty of having a model is that whatever your decision, you will know why you have made that decision. If you decide to stay in a relationship, it will give you something to work toward. If you decide to leave, you will do so with less doubt. Using the parameters will help you build up the ability to see your partner clearly, whatever the course you choose. That is the best insurance policy you can have for future happiness.

Real Freedom: Becoming an Authority

When I was very young, I would spend the weekends at my grandmother's house. She lived in the Bronx, only a few miles from our apartment in Manhattan. But it might as well have been another country. The musty buildings were frayed around the edges. People had strange habits, like drinking seltzer water from blue glass bottles with metal nozzles, delivered each week in wooden boxes. There was a strong, if informal, sense of community. Neighbors would call out to each other from window to window. What was most striking to me was the fact that if I did something wrong, any adult in the neighborhood would feel quite free to admonish me. When I once pushed another little kid, a woman sitting on a wooden folding chair in front of the building grabbed me by the scruff of the neck and screamed at me in front of everyone. The other adults, looking at me sternly, did not question her action. These women had no problem asserting their authority around children.

Contrast this with today's world. Not only do adults avoid disciplining the children of others, they often don't even discipline their own. They lack confidence in their authority as parents. The children pay a terrible price for this failing because, without authority, adults cannot give children what they need. Love is not enough. Children lack the experience and perspective to deal with the world around them. The role of the parent is to guide children by actively setting limits and teaching them to restrain themselves. Without a strong inner sense of authority, this job is impossible. Children *feel* you more than they listen to you. They do not decide to accept what you tell them because it makes logical sense. They accept it only because they feel your authority in a positive way. If children do not sense that you are stronger than they are, you are useless to them as a parent. You have not prepared them to deal with reality and in that sense you have failed them.

One advantage of setting strong limits for children is that it prevents them from being involved in matters that are none of their affair. One time, a patient of mine was preparing to ask his two young children if they thought it would be a good idea for the family to have a third child. Shocked, I explained to him that children are ill-equipped to make such a decision. Worse, even asking them suggests they are participants in the adult world. This has two negative effects. First, it gives them too much power. Being children, they will almost always misuse this power to manipulate their parents and cause disharmony in the family. Second, it exposes them to the stresses of adult living long before they are strong enough to deal with them. Too much power and too much anxiety are spiritual poisons for children. Our responsibility is to keep them in the child's world until they are really strong enough to leave it. But that takes authority.

———

Why does the modern parent find it so hard to function as an authority? The answer lies in a paradox. In order to *wield* authority as an adult, it is first necessary to *submit* to authority as a child. If you think of authority as a force with which you must have a relationship, then depending on your age and situation, there is a correct way to have that relationship. The child's relationship to authority must be to submit to it. The adult's relationship to authority is to wield it. But if the adult has not formed this relationship properly during his childhood, he does not have a healthy feeling for authority and will be unable to comfortably assert himself. He will be too timid or too strident.

In the 1960s, many adopted the idea that kids could regulate themselves. They would know when to go to sleep, what to eat, how much TV to watch. The result was a generation of children who never learned to submit to authority. It was this generation who were largely unable to be strong parents. Yet the impulse behind the changes of the sixties was positive; it stemmed from a tremendous desire for freedom and individuality. But the model for becoming a free individual was a defiant one, and defiance as an organizing principle shows its weaknesses over time.

True individuality can only be gained through discipline and submission. Not submission to an individual, but to a higher form of authority that is presented to us in the specific demands of life itself. If you submit to this higher authority, you can then become an authority yourself. This type of selfhood takes more work but carries an inherent power that others can feel. It not only commands respect, it inspires others. This higher form of selfhood is the only real freedom. It will serve you, not only as a parent, but as a friend, employer, or community leader. No matter what your childhood was like, there are specific ways you can develop this higher inner authority:

Forward Motion in Your Life

True authority must emanate from who you are. It is not possible to fake it. Those around you sense the depth of your life experience and will respect you accordingly. The notion of forward movement means that you continue to have new experiences in the world and deeper experiences of yourself. This constant motion makes you alive. Young people will instantly feel if you have this expanding sense of life or not. If you find yourself without spiritual direction, without interest in anything creative, without involvement in a community, without deep relationships, you are not moving forward. This developing of new capacities in yourself requires the same discipline and submission that are so crucial for children. Controlling your personal habits and fulfilling the responsibilities of your daily life strengthen your sense of inner authority.

Tolerating Misunderstanding

A true authority expresses herself independently of what others think. You develop this ability by holding your position even when you have no external support or your intentions are fundamentally misunderstood. We all have a childish need to be validated and adored by those around us. As painful as it feels, the experience of being misunderstood or disliked forces you to function emotionally as an adult.

Living by Higher Values

A defiant approach to gaining individuality can have a negative impact on society because it usually lacks any reference to a higher value that would benefit people outside oneself. It is rare that you hear any special interest groups in Washington, D.C., allude to the effects of their demands on the rest of society. Authority comes to those who find and express higher values. It takes a lot of work to do this in our daily lives, particularly with children. It means you have to make sure that each time you intervene to correct their behavior, you are being guided by a set of values, such as respect, discipline, love, generosity. Without certain values, your leadership is disorganized and reactive. Commitment to higher values must be real; you must live by the values yourself. "Do as I say, not as I do" erodes your credibility instantly.

The drive for individual freedom can't be reversed. Nor should it. There is no going back to the way things were even twenty years ago. But this drive does not have to destroy respect for authority in the young and willingness to wield authority in the old. The future of society depends on everyone consciously developing authority within themselves. The days of authority residing in a select few are over. (Witness, for instance, how medical information available on the internet has affected patients' relationships with their doctors.) It is only when everyone has developed their own authority that there will be a true community of equals. In this community, it will be impossible to fulfill one's duty to others *without* becoming an authority. Every single individual will make a difference. It is the responsibility of all of us to create this future. But you can only start with yourself.

Our Most Wasted Natural Resource: Words of the Wise

I once treated a man in his thirties who had gotten himself into big trouble. His law firm was handling the buyout of an electronics company by a much larger competitor. While the deal was still secret, he disclosed it to a journalist friend. No one did any illegal trading, but his firm found out that he had leaked confidential information. He was given the option of resigning. If he refused, they threatened to open a formal SEC investigation. My patient was a rising star in the firm. Smoking fat cigars and wearing fancy suits, he was almost a caricature of a young person's view of power. Now he faced a devilish choice. Resignation would mean losing the status to which he was addicted. If he tried to bluster his way through the charges, he could end up being convicted of a felony.

This man was raised by a father who was equally bright and articulate, a businessman who had also been successful at an early age. Headstrong, the father had ignored good advice and overexpanded. His business went bankrupt and he was left with huge debts. He abandoned his wife and son, moved to Florida, and led a very limited life as a night watchman. The son hated him for leaving, and most of all, for failing.

In the midst of his dilemma, my patient became depressed and paralyzed. He was aware enough to see the parallel between his life and his father's. I suggested he consult his father, with whom he hadn't spoken in years. A phone call led to a quick trip to Florida, where he found his seventy-year-old father living in one room. Once larger than life, he was now humble and quiet as a mouse. To the son, he was literally not the same person. What shocked the son most was that his father grasped his situation instantly and was quite eloquent in convincing him to resign. Years later, the wisdom of this decision was borne out. The son avoided disbarment and a criminal record. When he regained his success, he no longer had to wear it on his sleeve.

This case was one in a thousand. Usually, the opposite happens. We go about our adult lives rarely consulting our parents. In fact, we rarely consult anyone whom we consider "old" as a source of guidance. Thus a priceless natural resource is wasted. It is the equivalent of watching a business fail while you have a bank account from which you refuse to draw funds. This is not to say that all parents can help their adult children. Nor does it imply your parents know better than you. But to assume that the sum total of their life experience is worthless is absurd. Worse, it has destructive spiritual effects.

- A rift widens between the generations. In our culture, each generation struggles intensely to free itself from its forebears. As an adolescent, you need to feel that your parents don't know anything. You gain your first sense of selfhood by defying those on whom you were dependent. Your ego wants to feel that it can shape its own destiny, that it "knows" enough to succeed in life on its own, independent of any higher power. Becoming an adult is the process of destroying this attitude as you encounter forces that are bigger than your own will. The spiritual function of a society is to offer wisdom and support when the individual ego has failed. Older people have a special role to play at those times, and accepting their wisdom is exactly what keeps them connected to us. A society that rejects older adults is cutting off its own head.

• Ignoring older people implies that the sum total of a human life is nothing. In the ancient world, the most priceless possession was the wisdom gained through a long life. It was considered impossible to be wise without the depth of that experience. This was *living wisdom*. Today, we worship intellectual knowledge that is abstract and can be mastered at almost any age. Young people running mutual funds now manage a huge portion of the assets in the United States. They have excellent technical training but have been through few or no sustained financial crises. It will be interesting to see how they react when the inevitable crisis comes. Even more damaging, we long to hear the opinions of twenty-four-year-old athletes and celebrities because we have substituted fame for true wisdom, an abdication of responsibility that is truly frightening. There is a natural form and rhythm to a human life. This doesn't mean that every life should be the same, but in rough terms, we all go through the same phases. As you live, you are creating something. The ancients sensed this. They felt that over the course of a long life, we are shaped by God, just as God shapes a tree. For them, the elders were more complete, more valuable. We have left this view behind. We subject older people to a perverse model; at the exact time a person has achieved real wisdom, we take his voice away.

- Rejecting our elders creates fear and self-hatred in the young. On some level we realize that we will, someday, be old. We also know this is a society where shame is associated with old age. This view makes every day that passes a failure instead of a blessing. The result is thinking that we must experience accomplishment right now rather than over the course of our lives. Our general bad habits of hyperactivity, competitiveness, and envy get worse. By their late forties, people begin to actively hate themselves for aging. Without the belief that we are living the totality of a God-willed life, no amount of money or fame will calm us down.

The special role older adults play in society goes far beyond the fact of their life experience; they actually live in a different space from the rest of us. Our physical bodies, with their drives and desires, are in one sense an obstacle to spiritual experience. You can see this most clearly in people in their twenties, when there is almost an obsession with physical experience. At this age we are very closely bound up with the material world, and we should be. The aged, even those who are not physically ill, are in the opposite position. They are still here but without the degree of attachment younger people have. Like small children, they are closer to God. But unlike children, they have the ability and experience to communicate their wisdom to us. They can look at things from a higher point of view without the egotism and fear that cloud judgment. That is why they were venerated by the ancients.

It is actually not very hard to get older folks to open up. It is a mistake to assume that because they may offer very little, they have nothing to offer. But because of society's attitudes, they rarely feel it is their place to voice an opinion about the lives of their grown children. They must be *asked*. Their emotional situation is more fragile than younger people want to admit. Even those with money feel increasingly irrelevant. When children are growing up, parents seem to have a God-like power. Once we are grown, we tend to forget that these same parents now feel powerless and in fact are usually terrified of doing anything to alienate their children. It makes no difference how strong, or even abusive, they were thirty years ago. Their essential condition now is one of neediness. It is the responsibility of the child to take the initiative to start up a dialogue. It is the rare case where the parent won't be willing to open up, to the degree they are able. And so creating a line of communication with your parent, or any other older person, must be an active process, with the younger person initiating the connection. Not only will you be rewarded with the accumulated wisdom of a long life, but by making the effort, you will be developing a spiritual power in yourself that is capable of the following.

You will heal your own family. If you make the effort, it will be obvious how changed the dynamics of power are between you and your parents, and how vulnerable your parents are to their adult children. You will also be able to get something from them that has value to you in the present. It will be easier to forgive your parents their mistakes of years ago.

You will contribute to generational harmony. Each effort you make toward an older person helps to heal the rift that impoverishes our whole society. Young and old were meant to live together.

You will create a new value system for yourself. Your older parent is the future you. How you treat them reveals how you feel about your own future, which, I assure you, will be as an older person. Valuing the wisdom of your parents teaches you to view the passage of time as the natural expression of an alive universe, not something to fear or deny.

Only then will you be at peace with yourself.

What Children Need

Everyone wants the best for their children. But how best to achieve it? No question evokes more anxiety among parents. The world looks like a fast-moving train filled with high-status jobs, social acceptance, fame, and wealth. What if your child misses the train?

The panic begins early, with parents desperate to get their child into certain preschools and grade schools, all inevitably leading to the best universities—trying to make sure their child will end up a member of some favored class. Despite yourself, your voice takes on a nervous, pleading quality at the preschool interview that will determine the fate of your two-year-old. An inner voice tells you this is a world gone mad. *Will rejection from the right kindergarten really ruin my child's life?*

The fear comes from the illusion that there is something *out there* that will assure your child's future. And that this thing—the right friends, the right school, whatever it may be—will enable your child to like herself, be respected by others, and be safe from the unpredictable events of life (events that you were unable to avoid). The illusion assumes a magical power, an allure that causes everyone to compete fiercely. What you are doing is seeking ultimate value in the *out there*. You are in the world of fear, and it is no place to raise a child.

If you buy into this illusion, you're affecting your child deeply whether she wins or loses. No matter what you say in words, you're sending her the following messages.

- You accept the values and solutions of the herd without seriously questioning them. You do not trust your own instincts.
- It's not how you live that matters, but where you end up. You have placed your faith in status.
- Something *out there,* something outside the family, is more important than the family itself. You are devaluing the family.

The last is the most damaging. Once the family is devalued, your child has lost something priceless, something she cannot get anywhere else. The horrifying effects of weakened families are sometimes all too obvious, but sometimes more difficult to see, depending on the outward image a specific family wants to portray to its community. (By the way, when I say *family,* I mean it to include single parents and any other combination of adults responsible for raising children.)

How do you develop the strength and confidence to make your own family of primary importance, to know that what you're teaching your child is of fundamental, irreplaceable value? The parent has to find a way to say, "Wait, whatever we are doing in our family, that is what's most important to my child—not who their friends are or what school they go to." Understand, though, this task is not a conceptual one. You are trying to build the family as a living thing, something your child can experience every day. Only then can you build a base so strong that nothing in the outer world can overcome it. This is what your child needs from you. And only this will allow you to feel satisfied with yourself as a parent.

To build something this strong, you need a consistent philosophy that embodies the values that your family stands for. Only deeply held values, practiced every day, can make something come alive. There are three things that are indispensable for a strong family: love, spirituality, and discipline. These values turn the family into a secure place, which is the opposite of the world of fear. They are inner, they are universally available, and they are not subject to scarcity or competition. They make the family come alive as a source of meaning. They will make your home a calmer, happier place and will help your child immeasurably. Your job as parent is to make every day meaningful to your child; that's why parenting is the hardest job in the world.

Love

Love exists only to the degree that it is being expressed. The more it is expressed, the more it grows. This must be taught to children through example. They need to learn that it is their responsibility to be loving, particularly to their siblings. They need to see their parents being loving toward each other every day. They particularly need to see love expressed by adults during times of great stress, during times of conflict, and during those times when the adults are burdened with tedious responsibilities. They need to learn that it takes work to love, and that the work of love is their job. If you think of love as a substance, then the highest responsibility of the family is to generate as much of it as possible. Being loving becomes a group task for the family.

Spirituality

Your child needs to see that you have a relationship with some higher power. This will not only make you stronger in her eyes, but at the same time will make you more human and accessible. This is not a theoretical issue with children. They are naturally closer to God than adults but will bury those feelings unless encouraged. This does not require the practice of an organized religion. What it does require is that you don't fake it. Any effort you make to create a spiritual connection for yourself creates an environment that gives your child permission to experience their own connection to God. They need this every day, at meals, at bedtime, as part of the day. Spirituality in the family lets children experience awe and harmony—priceless gifts.

Discipline

Discipline is the thread that weaves the family into something that is predictable to the child. Nothing can live without consistency, least of all the family. Children must be taught to respect time. This means that important things like going to sleep, eating, and bathing must be done when it is time to do them (preferably at the same time every day), not when the child feels like doing them. As a parent, you won't be able to run the family this way unless you have the will to run your own life in an organized way. Children must be taught that controlling impulses is an accomplishment. When a child is prevented from eating a second doughnut, she will feel deprived. But it is from temporary experiences of deprivation that the child gains everything. The outer world is conquered and her inner soul lights up. By letting her have everything, she ends up with nothing.

These are dynamic forces that create tangible results. But it is up to you to make them dynamic. Believing in them conceptually is not enough. Espousing them verbally is not enough. You must live them. As a parent, nothing you do is innocuous.

These values create a wellspring of inner strength that allows your child to go on through rejection and adversity. They give her the courage to express herself. They make her strong enough to form her own opinions. Without these values, the journey of life will be miserable even if she "wins." They'll also help you resist pushing your child ahead too quickly. As a society, we often tend to focus on the development of the intellect above all else (early reading is a good example). Prior to first grade, children need to live in their own world, in a world of fantasy. This is not supposed to be a period of achievement, but a time when the child is drawing tremendous strength from this other world, strength that will be tangible later on in life.

There is one other thing your child needs from you. She needs you to continue to develop as a person. Part of creating a family that is truly alive is being alive yourself.

Everything that is alive is growing.

Everything.

The moment you feel there is nothing more for you to learn, that you have no personal challenges that mean anything, a part of you dies. This dead part then becomes a burden on your child. She will either withdraw from you, or will attempt to make up for your lack of effort through her own success. Either way is a disaster. If you keep yourself in motion as a person, you become light. Your own movement illuminates the world for the child.

Then you have given your child the ultimate gift—yourself.

What Teenagers Need

This has been a shocking era in the nation's schools. We have read, again and again, about teenagers who bring firearms to class and murder students and teachers. Simple explanations don't apply. Of course, mental health, easy access to guns, and violence in all forms of media are contributory factors, but they alone don't explain why some particular kids enact this horror. Years ago, I watched a reporter interview several kids who had brought guns to school, trying to understand how they could have reached a state of such utter disregard for the lives of others. The adolescents seemed remarkably disassociated from their actions, saying things like, "I was there and I wasn't there," "I guess reflex took over," and "Killing just felt cool." What they were describing was a dark force that had completely overcome them, destroying whatever morality and self-restraint we normally associate with being human.

The pull of that dark force is very strong in teenagers. We all have this part of our psyche, an inner demon that wants us to be special, above the rules, and not part of a holistic universe. As I said earlier, I call it Part X. In adolescents, it expresses itself in their attraction to a counter-world that defies adults and most specifically defies their own families. Drug abuse and all-around sullenness are some results of its influence. Parents of teenagers palpably feel this force emanating from their children like some mysterious black cloud they are helpless to combat. But you can understand this force and become a counterforce with real power to help your child.

Teenagers aspire to freedom above all else. They want to separate from their parents and experience their own individuality. True freedom is only acquired through a long process that requires courage and discipline. But teenagers, still basically children, mistake a false form of freedom for the real thing. This false freedom feels much more powerful to them, at least in the short term. This is the genius of Part X. It uses immediate physical gratification to make its point. In effect, the message is "If I can give you such a strong physical experience (through drugs, sex, rage, etc.), then the rest of what I tell you must be true."

But the rest of what Part X suggests is a lie. It says freedom is the ability to avoid reality. Real freedom is exactly the opposite. It is developed through submission to the three inescapable aspects of reality: pain, uncertainty, and effort. Part X tempts teenagers with the idea that it's not "fair" that they should have to put up with all this discomfort. They have the "right" to avoid the unpleasant aspects of reality. Impulsive gratification is just the trick.

Once a parent gets a feeling for this force, she can see a lot of disparate adolescent behavior as part of one whole. In many cases, the behavior has nothing to do with how the

WHAT TEENAGERS NEED | 99

child was raised. It is an independent and inevitable product of the desire to leave childhood. But that doesn't mean it should remain unchallenged. When adolescents act out and participate in adult activities, forces in their personalities are activated at too early an age and don't develop to their fullest later on. These forces must be held back in adolescence to build strong adults.

But why should they hold back? Moral discussions are rarely convincing to kids. They must grasp the concept that using restraint and being part of a structure will make them stronger and give them real power. In times past, church, school, and community had a strong influence on behavior. There were outer moral strictures that applied to everybody. Our present society has failed in that we no longer provide a credible reason why kids should control themselves. In the broader society, no one seems to be controlling themselves. The drive for individuality and freedom in our society has gutted institutions of their authority. No one wants to accept an arbitrary set of rules. This need not be a disaster if it causes each of us to construct an inner model of self-control in which we are responsible for ourselves. This is actually the true meaning of freedom. But unlike arbitrary morality, it cannot be imposed from the outside, not even from a parent. The only thing a parent can do is develop a force in himself that offers an alternative to the false, lower form of freedom. This higher form of freedom may not have coercive power over your child, but it has a depth and constancy that they can feel and that will influence them over time. This force cannot be faked. It requires that the adult actually change himself. The most ineffective thing a parent can do is to live in his own non-spiritual, undirected funk, and come out of it occasionally to yell at his teenager. The dishonesty of this actually makes a child even more determined to defy you. Ninety percent of communication with your child is nonverbal; they can sense if this higher force is present.

Whether you're a married or single parent, it is possible to function in a way that makes the family structure more real and credible to a teenager. The challenge is to make the family a living thing with a set of values. The teenager will still rebel against it, but they will be making mental notes, aware of the power of the family. Even small improvements in yourself will subtly change your interactions with your teenager. There has been a loss of will and confidence on the part of adults to assert their own value system with adolescents. You have a vast and superior knowledge to offer your teenager. The best way to communicate that knowledge is to live it yourself. Higher freedom can be developed in the following ways.

Renunciation

Asking a kid to give up harmful pleasures when you can't give them up yourself is hollow and engenders hate. Pick one bad habit and work on it immediately. It's the effort that counts; you don't have to be perfect. Drop from two packs to five cigarettes a day and you'll feel a new force in yourself when you talk with your child. Renouncing certain pleasures is not a moral act, nor should it be self-punishing or ascetic. It is the specific exercise of freedom. In this case, you are freeing yourself from your own Part X with its compulsive desires. Kids think freedom means going deeper into the material world and its immediate gratification. Remember that real freedom means being freed from the material world.

Discipline

I mentioned discipline in the last chapter as it relates to small kids, but to go further, you have to live according to an invisible structure that has regularity to it. This includes when you go to sleep and wake up, when you eat meals, when you exercise, when you pray. The rhythm this brings into your life has a real force to it. Teenagers tend to think that the mark of freedom is the right to do whatever you want, whenever you want to. In reality, that makes you a slave to your impulses. Those in the arts most easily accept this, since without discipline, they would not have the power to express themselves creatively. When you live according to an invisible structure, you bring higher forces to bear on whatever you are trying to accomplish. These forces give you true freedom.

Forward Motion

The universe is alive and moving. You must continue to expand and move forward in your own life to stay in touch with this life force. The terms of this vary from person to person. It could involve creative projects, service to the community, career change, spiritual development, etc. Forward motion is a lifelong responsibility for all of us. If you allow yourself to shrink away from the world, a part of you dies. Remember, Part X constantly offers adolescents its version of what it feels like to be alive and does so in a compelling, stimulating manner. A parent who is half dead herself does not have the credibility to challenge this lie.

Your authority, wisdom, and goodness as a parent will constantly be shaken and challenged during your child's adolescence. And there are some teenagers who cannot be reached at all. None of these solutions are magic. This model tends to pick up steam the longer you can stick to it. It requires faith to work on yourself as an individual during a period of crisis with your child. No matter how much one might wish it, there is no going back to the time when authorities were respected merely because of their position. The challenge now is to make the family and community alive with real higher powers.

Only this will command true respect from the young.

Knowing by Doing

In the early eighties I watched something very special come to life: The Wellness Community. This unique organization offered psychological and spiritual support to those with life-threatening illnesses, all at no charge. Like most great things, it started with a few people sitting around a room talking. The group consisted of the initiator of the idea, Harold Benjamin, and five therapists who were experienced in treating cancer survivors. Harold was in his fifties, and had been so successful as a real estate lawyer that he had retired and dedicated himself to good works. He had brought in the therapists (including me) to advise him on how to create the Community. Harold was tightly wound, abrasive at times, and lacked formal training in psychology. It was easy for us to look down at him, shielded by our credentials, and explain how difficult it was going to be to realize his vision.

Within a few weeks, it was clear that Harold should have been advising us. At each meeting, one or two good ideas would surface. The professionals would then discuss the ideas in a critical manner until they beat them to death. Paralysis would fill the room. Inevitably, Harold would snap us out of our stupor by taking action on an idea, right then and there. He would simply pick up the phone and make a call. Because I had been trained in a rigid medical environment, this behavior was a revelation to me. Each time he reached for the phone I could feel the room tense up, each of us thinking, "You just can't do that." But he did. By the end of each meeting, he'd have a speaker or a consultant lined up or a new program on the schedule. Little by little, The Wellness Community took shape.

I witnessed the act of something being created. We therapists could never have done it ourselves because we needed to feel each step was the "right" step. We needed to feel certain before we could act. But nothing new can be brought into the world in a state of complete certainty. Creating requires you to go into the unknown. Harold could act before he knew if he was doing the right thing. Dynamic individuals all have this ability. It is a faith in taking action. They have this faith because they sense that the information they need does not come from thinking, it comes from the action itself. I call this intelligence of the will. It means your will is not just an energy that enables you to do things, it is also a perceptive force—almost like a sense organ.

This is a radical notion for our society. We view intelligence as a dried-out thought process that goes on inside our heads. But that's only the lower form of intelligence, called knowing. Higher intelligence is called wisdom. It's not inside your head, it's spread out in the world around you. The will to take action connects you to this world of wisdom.

The ancients thought of the entire universe as one live organism woven through and through with the intelligence of the gods. We think we know better. We "know" the universe to be a random collection of objects, some given life through a biochemical accident. But we pay a price for that arrogance—a terrified paralysis in the face of the unknown.

If wisdom is out there, then the only way we can gain it is by taking action. The will is more intelligent than the process of thinking. Let's say we're planning to open a doughnut shop. We could spend hundreds of hours debating what percentage of the doughnuts should be chocolate and what percentage vanilla. If we take the action of opening the shop, we will learn more about how many of each flavor to make in one day than we could in a year of abstract thinking. The world of doughnut eaters will give us the information we need.

To act in the face of the unknown brings up a primal fear in most of us. You can overcome this fear if you learn to look at action in a new way. Here are three principles that make the process of taking action more effective.

Speed

Once you have determined to do something, the less time you allow to elapse until you act, the better. A failed action, done quickly, will improve your confidence more than one done after great procrastination, even if it succeeds.

Density

Dynamic people take more actions in one morning than most people take in a month. The goal is to take many more actions in a given time period than you normally do. Start slowly, try to take even just two actions in a day, and increase from there.

Nightly Review

Reserve ten minutes before bed to review, in writing, the actions taken during the day and the ones you want to commit to for tomorrow. Anything written down becomes more serious, and you are less likely to lie to yourself about how much you've done.

If you practice this new philosophy of action, you will begin to feel the value of every action you take. Start with small steps until this philosophy becomes your natural way of functioning. If you stick to it, you will experience an influx of wisdom that will guide you very practically to your next step. The fact that you learn as much from the failures as the successes will teach you that the result of any given effort is not important. The only thing that matters is that you continue the process.

This philosophy of action solves a fundamental problem of motivation in people who tend to be inert and have a low life force. That's because intelligence of the will associates wisdom with action, which is alive, rather than with thinking, which is dead. Some people slouch into my office and complain that they would become motivated if only they knew what they were supposed to do. They wait passively for some magic experience that will give them a sense of direction. Not only does this never happen, but it shows a complete misunderstanding of motivation. I always suggest that they take action now, no matter how unsure they feel about their current path. This exercise of the will increases their life force. It is the life force itself, not their reasoning ability, that will allow a person to discover what their new direction should be. It is foreign to us to think of the life force as a perceptive force with its own intelligence. But have you ever seen someone who is very alive who lacks a sense of direction?

You will begin to look at goals differently, too. Since the information you need comes from the process of taking action, then the function of goals is to stimulate that process. There is no such thing as a right goal or a rational goal. Start with goals that are available to you right now. All goals are temporary. Once you commit through action, your life force increases and will bring with it the intelligence to form your next goal.

The intelligence of the will leads to a spiritual view of action. Whether we're in touch with it or not, each of us has a part that wants to ceaselessly move forward and create. This is our immortal part, the higher self. It is connected to a higher life that fills us with wisdom and makes us indifferent to temporary failure. The goal of modern spirituality is to not withdraw the higher self from the world. Rather, it should express itself. Taking action to gain wisdom is actually a way to activate and experience your higher self. This means that everyone's life journey is important. Every step matters.

Welcome to the Club:
We're All Insecure

I mentioned this phenomenon more generally earlier in the book, but to be specific: I once watched a mother pull strings, call in favors, quite literally beg for the privilege of paying tens of thousands of dollars for her child's kindergarten. Normally passive and insecure, this patient of mine turned into Superwoman when it came to getting her son into an exclusive private school. She came from a family she freely described as "trailer trash." Her ticket out was physical beauty, which allowed her to make a living in the city as a model. She married a guy who loved her but never became as successful as she hoped. She was tortured by the idea that there was a level of society she had not reached, a level where everyone was completely secure. She had given up the hope of ever getting there herself and focused all this ambition on her son. The private school was to be the door into this elite world and nothing was going to stop her from getting him through it. Everything went according to plan until school started.

As she walked him into school each morning, she became certain that the other mothers were giving her the cold shoulder and looking at her in a funny way. Rarely would any of them come up and talk. She quickly concluded that she was not good enough for them. The sense of rejection made her self-critical, particularly about her looks, the only thing that had ever made her feel confident. Months later on a class outing, she finally made friends with two women who told her that, in truth, the other mothers had felt shunned by her. What they saw was a disdainful, strikingly attractive female striding past them each day without so much as a second glance. She made them feel incredibly insecure.

What shocked this woman most was not that she had misjudged the situation. It was the fact that the other women could feel insecure at all. In her eyes, they were charter members of a superior class of Range Rover–driving goddesses who could not possibly have flaws of their own. It took her months more to recognize a fundamental law of human nature: everyone thinks there's something wrong with them. Everyone has a part of themselves they don't want to reveal to the world because they see it as inferior. Carl Jung, the Swiss psychiatrist, called this the shadow. He defined it as the part of yourself you wish didn't exist but somehow can't get rid of.

This woman could easily accept the fact that she had a shadow. It was her secret sense of contamination by her shiftless family. She was afraid she could never get far enough away from them and that someday her membership in this clan would be exposed. But it was hard for her to believe that the highbred women at the school had anything to be ashamed of. They seemed to have everything. But everyone has something that makes them feel inadequate—a secret addiction, a lack of physical perfection, increasing age, the fact of not finishing college. We all project the sum total of these weaknesses onto our inferior alter ego, the shadow.

Then we try to hide our shadow from the world. It's like putting all your failings into a bag and stuffing it into your closet. The result is that in some way or another, we avoid the world and hide behind a facade. We show people only the parts of ourselves we've determined are acceptable. That's why so many people feel like frauds. My patient wanted to believe a supergroup existed who did not have shadows. She could thus hope to make her son a member. Accepting the impossibility of this was the beginning of growing up for her. It was a realization that changed the goal of living from getting rid of the shadow to accepting it.

But what good is it to accept your weaknesses and failings? The answer is that they lead you to accept the reality of your human condition. No matter how specific the things are that you feel ashamed of, they are never the ultimate reason that you feel inferior.

Inferiority is the basic spiritual condition of man.

Even members of the most elite groups feel inferior. In Western culture, this is called the Fall of Man. In a mythological sense, it means we have fallen out of an immortal state, paradise, into the frail, temporary, messy condition of living in a physical body. We are living inside instruments that are rotting away on a daily basis. No matter how glorious your outer achievements, they will be temporary. Your shadow is the part of you that knows this truth, no matter how hard you try to cover it up. Mythologically, it is your higher self that remembers your original higher state in paradise and thus knows how far you have fallen. The higher self has put on your failings like it would a suit of clothes, thus creating the shadow. In a sense, it has sacrificed itself to become a mirror in which you can see the truth about yourself, which is that you are, of course, a flawed human being. The shadow is not really the inferior part of you, it is merely the witness to the truth of your human condition. The shadow is the higher self in disguise. In Western mythology, the story of Christ best reflects this dynamic. Christ represented the shadow of the entire human race.

People will do anything to keep their shadow hidden. They live in a limited world where they are afraid to express themselves. They avoid meeting new people, they fear intimacy, they can't take a creative risk. They can't confront their boss or speak in public. Some feel so inferior, they can't even write down their own thoughts in a private journal. They don't understand the real nature of the shadow, and so it becomes an adversary.

But the shadow is really your greatest asset.

It is the unique, uninhibited child within you, the part that follows its instincts and is completely self-accepting. Our know-it-all egos have judged this part as inferior, when it is actually a source of higher forces that can literally create magic. Your insecurities become opportunities. The more you accept your weaknesses, the more you activate these creative forces. That is the real power of self-acceptance. Understanding this also changes the purpose of life. You no longer go into the world to meet outer standards of success, but instead to reveal your shadow and learn to accept it. You are released from the tyranny of worrying about what others think of you and are free to express yourself.

Thinking about self-acceptance is not enough. You need tools to practice it. Here are three:

Make your shadow into a reality that you can experience.

It is possible to make things in your unconscious real by giving them a visual form. Close your eyes and take yourself back to a time in your life when you felt particularly injured, rejected, or alienated. It could be when you were humiliated in front of the other kids in grade school, when a relationship ended badly, or during a depressed period in college. See yourself at that age as if you are looking at another person. See the pain in that person's face. Be aware of the details of her appearance and demeanor. You are looking at your shadow. Now say to the shadow, "You are real, you will never go away, you are valuable." Take a moment to feel what it's like to be in the presence of your shadow. Practice this until you can re-create your shadow at will. This real part of you exists in the present and is available to help by generating creative forces.

Pay careful attention to your negative experiences.

They can have value if you process them properly. Each moment of hurt feelings, self-criticism, or inferiority represents the emergence of your shadow. Instead of fearing these moments, you should use them as cues to express love and acceptance to the shadow. Bring up a visual of the shadow and speak to it with the emotion you would have if it were your own child. Imagine yourself hugging it for a moment. The entire exercise takes less than ten seconds. You are systematically embracing your shadow. You will feel less afraid of the world and less inferior. Confidence will come as you integrate your shadow and accept yourself.

Force yourself into situations of self-expression that you would normally avoid.

Let's say you take yourself to a party filled with intimidating people. Being there will bring up a lot of the negative cues. This means you'll have to talk to your shadow throughout the evening. The focus will shift away from how others react to you, and toward the inner goal of deepening your bond with your shadow.

In the Middle Ages, alchemists searched for the mythological philosopher's stone, said to have magic transformative powers. The secret to finding the stone was that it was common, something no one would bother to pick up. Everyday negative experiences, especially of inferiority, are like the magic stone. Instead of transforming lead into gold, you are transforming yourself.

The meaning of life, with all its pain, becomes comprehensible when you realize that you go out into the world to develop a relationship with yourself.

Making Peace with Conflict

In my late twenties I became a student of karate to try to overcome my fear of physical confrontation. I liked my instructor, so when he moved the class to a boxing gym in the South Bronx, I followed him there. The gym was really an extension of a church that stood alone on the corner of a rubble-strewn block, every other building having been demolished. I can still feel the tension that filled me every time I drove over the bridge from Manhattan into this harsh landscape. The atmosphere inside the gym was even more intimidating, at least initially. Everyone else was from the Bronx. To them, training in karate or boxing was a deadly serious undertaking. A sense of controlled rage radiated from the men sparring in the center ring or hitting the heavy bags. They didn't show me mercy because I was a beginner. One guy used to make it a point to beat me up when we sparred and seemed to particularly hate me. But as the months wore on, I noticed that the intense emotion would dissipate by the end of the workout, replaced by a kind of loving peace that filled the room. The same guys who seemed so ready to kill each other an hour before became connected by some mysterious bond. When I left one night, I couldn't start my car. This was a tough neighborhood, and being stranded there after dark, I felt my familiar fear of a possible confrontation. Then from out of the shadows came the same guy who beat me up every workout. I wasn't sure what to expect, but all I saw on his face was concern. He arranged to have my car towed, then walked me safely through the streets to the subway, treating me like a family member. This world that had seemed so scary to me was suddenly full of love.

The bond connecting the men in the gym existed not in spite of the conflict and fighting, but because of it. This was an extreme example of the fact that there can be no deep connection between human beings without conflict. If you want to get close to someone, you must enter what I call the zone of engagement. This is the space where people get close enough to each other to become vulnerable. Vulnerability causes fear and fear leads to conflict. But if the conflict is handled properly, a real bond is created. Conflict becomes a kind of sense organ through which you really get to know another person. This zone of engagement is a dynamic place. A certain magic is created when humans get together. When you enter the zone, you get the following benefits.

- You feel truly connected to the world and to a sense of home.
- New ideas come from being in this place.
- On the deepest level, this zone is a spiritual place. We meet the spiritual world most

immediately through our relationships to
others.

Most people avoid real engagement. They hate conflict
so much that they end up asking much less from the world
than they should. One result is the paradox of the modern
person, profoundly isolated in the midst of so many new
technologies of communication. This isn't really surprising. Technology rarely helps us become really engaged.
More likely, we use it to avoid conflict and vulnerability.
Millions enter social media platforms hiding behind their
screen names. Email avoids face-to-face confrontation.
Text messages enable us to send messages without the fear
of a real-time conversation. Taken to an extreme, strong
feelings of disconnectedness may explain part of why an
adolescent is so cut off that he can walk into his school,
armed, with the intention of killing classmates.

Why are we so afraid of conflict that we're willing to live
limited lives? Because of an illusion. Everyone has a childish part of themselves that believes itself to be "good."
Since the universe should be "fair," then there should be no
reason for anyone to disagree with us or, God forbid, dislike us. Nonetheless, conflict occurs. It feels extreme and
undeserved. We are shocked and have no way to process it.
The shock is not a response to the specifics of the attack or
dispute, it is to the fact that someone doesn't adore us. We
can't believe that the other person completely misunder-
stands what a good person we are. "How could anyone

treat me like that . . . *me*?" Being hated or misunderstood shatters your image of yourself. That is why people will do anything to avoid conflict. But this avoidance puts the zone of engagement off limits, and life is lived less deeply.

Part of truly becoming an individual and an adult is to accept that conflict is a normal part of life that cannot be avoided. Conflict is necessary in making a connection to others and is therefore potentially wildly positive. But it takes work to bring out this potential and feel more connected to the world.

Most of us react to conflict by reflex, without a plan or any higher goal. What typically happens? Negative judgments about the other person circulate in an endless loop in our heads. "I can't believe he said that to me. Wait till I get ahold of him, I'm going to tell him . . . !" At the same time, you withdraw from the other person into a shell, which makes you sullen and cut off from the rest of the world as well. This reaction is as effective as turning a car against the direction of a skid; it makes the situation worse. During conflict more than any other time, you need to keep connected to a higher world that transcends your immediate circumstances. This higher world has forces that flow through you and calm you and give you courage. This is a world of limitless love where there is no judgment. The moment you judge or withhold, you fall down from that world like a rock. You lose your resources and end up feeling frustrated and impotent. You feel tied up in knots.

The forces pulling us out of the higher world during conflict are habitual and strong. That's why work is required. And the most effective tool to use is called active love, which I mentioned briefly at the start of this book. This kind of love requires using your will. Most of us have a naïve view of love as something that should come naturally and thus requires no effort. Active love allows you to generate love in circumstances when you normally get caught up in hate. The purpose is not to let other people run over you. In fact, the more aggressive you need to be with someone, the more you need to send them active love. That's where your power lies. Active love keeps you connected to unstoppable forces from the higher world. Here's how it works:

Concentration: Imagine love to be a substance spread around you everywhere. Feel yourself sucking this surrounding substance into your chest where it becomes concentrated. **Transmission:** Send this concentrated love toward the other person. If you are not in their presence, direct it toward an image of them in your mind. It's like completely exhaling a breath, holding nothing back. **Penetration:** This is the most important step. Don't just watch the love enter their body, feel it enter. For a moment you will be at one with them. At this point, you enter the higher world. The definition of love is that it accepts everything. If you can send love to someone you hate then you can embrace anything in life. You have experienced real love. Not until then can you activate the higher world. You don't have to see this as a moral issue. You're obeying the laws of the higher world just as you obey the laws of gravity—involuntarily, and for your own good.

The key to active love is to view love as a substance, not as a judgment. You can turn a hose on a car you hate and wash it just as well as a car you love. Using active love does not imply that you approve of the other person's actions. In fact, the other person is irrelevant. You are making a higher assertion that, even if attacked, you refuse to be taken out of the higher world and lose your sense of flow and connectedness. You are keeping yourself in a state where conflict cannot intimidate you. Then you are free to fully engage with the world.

This is a new way to look at conflict resolution. Compromising on the details of a dispute isn't enough to create a lasting bond between people. There will always be new details and new disputes. The key is that each participant processes his own fear and hate during every conflict. If each of them does this, it creates goodwill, the result of spiritual work done during difficult times.

Only this gives you the faith to stay connected to another person.

Winning by Losing

Vince Lombardi is the most revered football coach of all time. His Green Bay Packers had an unmatched winning record in the sixties. Known for his ability to inspire his players, he is still the role model for modern coaches. A demanding taskmaster, he literally insisted that his players win. Losing was not allowed. Legend has it that his motto was "Winning isn't everything, it's the only thing." Whether he actually said that or not, the statement has become immortal. It is now the defining concept for modern America. One of our gods was Michael Jordan. He had looks, intelligence, and charm. But what he was (and still is) worshipped for is his ability to win, without fail, under pressure. Huge companies paid anything to be identified with his image. If you go back and look at his commercials, they are slick, aesthetically beautiful tributes to the glory of victory.

The obsession with winning has distorted athletics. No one seriously questions this. Pro teams hire athletes with any sort of problem as long as they help them win. Olympic athletes regularly dose themselves with illegal substances to enhance their performance. In everyday life, normally sane parents attack the umpire at a T-ball game because their seven-year-old's team is losing.

If only sports were affected, maybe it wouldn't be so bad.

But unfortunately, the idea that winning is the highest good has been applied to all aspects of our lives. It has become our philosophy. The aforementioned parents frantically pressing to enroll their children in the right preschool so they'll get into Harvard; the corporate executive cooking his books so his quarterly earnings won't disappoint the Street; the studio executive ensuring his box office with stupidly violent films. They're not merely trying to succeed, they're obsessed. Winning has truly become "the only thing" for them. They are practitioners of a modern philosophy that dictates that nothing can be more important than winning.

This belief has entered our lives so deeply that we rarely question it. But we should. Because the more we focus on winning in a one-sided way, the more we lose. It has nothing to do with what we are trying to win at. The problem is the state of mind this philosophy puts us in. When you make winning an obsession, you become completely fixated on your goal, and it becomes a matter of life-or-death. Eventually, all of your attention is focused on some *thing* outside yourself, whether it be career, money, fame, or another person. This is the state of attachment. You know you are in this state when you spend a great deal of time thinking and worrying about the same thing. It's the state of attachment itself that is the real loss. The Buddhists consider it the source of all suffering.

What have we lost in this state of attachment? We've lost

the connection to anything larger than ourselves. That higher force in the universe that makes it into one meaningful whole, the one that human beings cannot be happy without a connection to . . . *this force does not exist in things.* Things are fixed, while this force is pure movement. The more focused we become on a thing, the further we get from the spiritual energies we need.

Even worse, without a connection to higher forces, society breaks down. When everyone is focused on winning, they are concerned only with themselves. This pulls us further and further apart. The winners have no concern for the losers. At the beginning of the twentieth century, humankind believed that, through science, they could "win" over the material world. There could be "scientific" solutions to all human problems, including social and economic problems. What really happened in this century was an outbreak of evil and murder unprecedented in world history. As humanity lost the sense of anything greater than its own ego, it lost all restraint and came close to destroying itself.

In this next millennium, we will either regain our connection to higher forces or we will perish. Only higher forces can move us beyond our personal needs and obsessions and inspire us to care about each other. These forces can't be legislated, purchased, or mass-produced. In this new era, individuals—one by one—will have to bring these spiritual energies into the world. The great paradox is that it is not winning, but losing, that reconnects us to higher forces. This is so antithetical to how we see the world that at first it seems insane. But if you focus not on what is lost but on the state that loss puts you in, it makes sense. In an attached state, you've made the thing you're obsessed with into your ultimate reality. Regardless of what that thing is, your attachment to it puts you into a world where there is nothing higher than a thing. Attachment traps you in this world without higher forces. Only if you lose the thing are you freed from this empty world. Only then can you enter an alive world made of spiritual forces, not objects. That's the secret of loss: it allows you to gain a whole world. The world of objects is a limited world. Your gain is my loss, we are rivals. The world of higher forces is infinite. Only then do we all win. This is collective success. Without it we go back to tearing each other apart.

Most of us fail to tap into this spiritual potential in our losses. We are so focused on winning we don't know how to lose. This is tragic. The average person will avoid or ignore loss as long as possible. When it finally overwhelms him, he becomes demoralized or even paralyzed. What he doesn't know how to do is embrace loss actively.

In order to do this, you need three things:

- Acceptance of the inevitability of loss as part of life
- Recognition of the possibility of gaining higher forces from losses
- The ability to process the experience right at the moment the loss occurs

You can convert the experience of losing a thing into the experience of gaining a whole new universe if you have a tool to process the loss. The tool depends on the fact that behind every loss you suffer, there lies an infinite force. It's the same force that creates everything in the universe. Whether you call it God or not, it requires loss and destruction so it can create anew. Every loss you experience is a chance to form a relationship with this higher force. Instead, we try to bargain with it—"You can take my job but not my wife." But that's putting the prime mover of the universe on the same level as man. You must give up bargaining and learn to surrender fully to this force.

The only way to do this is to be willing to lose everything.

That's the key.

To practice loss processing, close your eyes and focus on the thing you're attached to. It could be money, status, health, or whatever. Imagine grasping it tightly. Then, suddenly, let go of it and say to yourself, "I'm willing to lose this money." At the same time, feel yourself falling. The sensation should be pleasurable and freeing. It's as if you were clinging to a ledge and suddenly let go. As you fall, see the sun somewhere below you. Feel yourself fall right into the sun. When you hit its surface, feel your body burn up. Say to yourself, "I'm willing to lose everything." Since your physical body is the instrument with which you possess objects, when you lose it, you are truly losing everything. Feel this as a relief. You now find yourself in the very center of the sun. Because you have no physical body, you are free to radiate outward in all directions along with the sun's rays. As you do this, picture many other suns surrounding you, all radiating toward you. Feel peace and harmony spreading among them. Now, open your eyes, and be back in your body. Imagine that the sun is still inside your heart.

You will feel a power you could never experience by possessing a thing.

The whole process takes a minute.

This tool works to process a loss that's already occurred in your life, as well as to deal with the fear of a possible loss in the future. Either way, you are training yourself to be in a nonattached state. Nonattachment won't make you passive. It doesn't mean you don't care about achieving your goals. But because you can accept their loss, they no longer have an obsessive, life-or-death meaning. You're learning to stay in touch with a force bigger than your personal desires. Winning is no longer the only thing.

Only then can you be happy.

Learning from Your Dreams

Few people realize that it was the wisdom of a dream that spurred Francis of Assisi to change his life and become the most renowned saint of all times, a man revered throughout the world by people of all denominations. Not many of us will achieve the greatness that Saint Francis did, but there is much we can learn from his story. His accomplishments are amazingly relevant today. The medieval society in which Francis lived was rotting. The ruling elite governed for their personal gain, leaving most of the populace impoverished. There were constant wars among the city-states. Minorities and the disabled were persecuted ruthlessly. Into this corruption, Francis introduced an astounding force of love and healing. But first, he had to undergo a transformation.

Francis was born rich and grew up to be a playboy, spending his father's money and courting beautiful women. But his real love was making war. While still quite young, he had already performed bravely in battle. Once, before a new campaign, Francis had a dream where he was in a palace where weapons and shields were stored. He took this to mean he should continue his career as a soldier. But in the middle of the expedition, he had a keen intuition that he had misinterpreted the dream and should return to Assisi.

Back home, the same inner voice brought the realization that the weapons in the dream were *spiritual* weapons of mercy, compassion, and love. After this, Francis became very ill. When he recovered, he found that his desire for physical conquest was transformed into the desire to spread peace and goodness. The man who dreamed of knightly glory walked destitute among the most despised of his society, the lepers.

Francis was able to turn away from a blindly materialistic path with the guidance of higher forces that appeared in a dream. For him, and others in the ancient world, these forces were considered spiritual. Today we, believing ourselves to be sophisticated, call them unconscious forces.

The forces that come to us in dreams have an undeniable power, a power we desperately need. But dreams are quite foreign to the state of mind we're used to. We must prepare ourselves to receive and understand them. There are many types of dreams. Some represent the desire to fulfill a wish, some represent fear of a future event, some even represent a physical sensation we may be experiencing, like heat. But these dreams are like the sounds of an orchestra warming up before it begins to play. They are noise without a higher purpose.

The dreams that are important are those that convey wisdom. They often come at key turning points in our lives. The modern world confuses wisdom with facts because facts are easy to come by. We are drowning in facts. But no amount of facts can guide us in the crucial moments of life.

What is right for one person given a set of facts will be wrong for another. Wisdom is a higher force that reveals where you as an individual need to go at a given moment. It is a bridge between you and the universe. Wisdom transcends the abilities of normal human thought. It lets you move forward with a sense of purpose.

Yet, the truth is, we resist wisdom. The ego thinks it knows, and doesn't like to be open to anything wiser than itself. So we stay in our ruts, seeing things the same old way. Usually we fixate on some outer goal, like career or status, and actively shut out anything that might distract us. We are one-sided.

That's where dreams come in.

The function of dreams is to correct your attitude. This was first stated by Carl Jung, who developed a comprehensive new way to deal with dreams. For example, we all have dreams of going to class or taking an exam at school, and invariably we're late or haven't studied. This represents the resistance of the ego to the "course" of emotional or spiritual study. We actually have to learn to become whole. The meaning of other dreams is not quite so obvious. As horrifying as they are, dreams in which you are being attacked or killed have nothing to do with physical danger. What is being attacked is your attitude. The dream is breaking down your fixation with the material world to allow you to become balanced. If you are having dreams like this frequently, open yourself to the possibility that there is a message you need to receive. You can even ask (before you go to sleep) for a dream that will clarify the message.

Being open to your dreams isn't enough. They come from a world with its own set of laws. If you view dreams the way you do everyday life, you will misunderstand the messages. Here are five key elements of dreams.

Symbolism

Dreams are basically pictorial, not verbal. And, like the weapons in Francis's dream, the images stand for things other than themselves. We like to believe that the highest form of intelligence is in words. That is a conceit of the ego; the ego thinks in words. In the ancient world, it was accepted that wisdom came in the form of images. The gods thought in images. Higher truths clothe themselves in images taken from everyday human life. That's why spiritual weapons were presented to Francis in the guise of the weapons he actually used. Jung discovered that certain symbolic patterns are universal, meaning that everyone is born with them in their unconscious. The symbols appear not only in dreams but in myths and works of art. He called these archetypes. An example is Darth Vader from Star Wars. Show a Star Wars film anywhere in the world, and the audience will recognize Vader on sight as the archetype of Evil. There are archetypes for the Mother, Father, God, and more. When archetypes appear, it means the dream is

connecting you to what Jung called the collective unconscious. This is a part of you that transcends your individual
history (which is the personal unconscious) and connects
you to a universal consciousness. Ancient humanity would
more simply call it the spiritual world.

Interactivity

Normally we think of symbols as static images or figures
that we view from the outside, like mathematical symbols.
Dream images are different. They are alive; they don't stand
still. You actually walk among symbols and interact with
them. In a dream, you may end up being chased by a symbol or find yourself eating it. When the dreamer reacts to
these living symbols as if they were objects in the real world,
he tends to misinterpret their meaning. You might see a
gold coin and greedily put it in your pocket. Instead of rep-
resenting material wealth, the coin is a symbol of wisdom.

Recurrence

When the dream world has an important message for you,
it will create a series of dreams on the topic. Sometimes
they occur night after night. Jung felt that the dreamer is
confronted over and over until he accepts the guidance. But
we become confused because dreams will tackle the same
issue in totally different ways. The need to be creative might
be represented by giving birth, but also by working in a gar-

den. The need to develop personal power may be represented by meeting with the president, but also by building up your muscles in a gym. This unwillingness of the dreamworld to pin itself down to one way of giving a message is disturbing to the ego, which likes things in a fixed form.

Innerness

Dreams are a paradox—you are taken to another world, yet that world is inside of you. If you are open, you can get a glimpse of your inner reality and the truths you normally deny. In dreams, you meet parts of yourself as if they were separate from you. A lion might represent your inner rage. A baby might stand for your higher self, which is born out of experience. Certain archetypes reveal hidden inner parts of the self. Your shadow, that Jungian inferior alter ego that most people try to hide, may appear as a beggar or as a person from your distant past whom you looked down on. As we know, facing and accepting your shadow is the first big step of inner growth.

Dramatic Structure

Dreams tend to tell their stories in three acts, much like movies. There is usually a setup, which often takes place in ordinary circumstances. Next there's a journey, a discovery, or a challenge. The setting usually becomes threatening or exotic or fantastic. That's when you have gone deeper into your psyche and entered the collective unconscious. The last act is about resolving your situation, perhaps returning home. The emotional ups and downs of a dream are a type of emotional education. In Greek drama, this was called *katharsis*.

Without question, the twenty-first century will focus on information. Science, logic, and computer-generated solutions certainly have a place. But they will never solve the deeper problems we face—how to accept loss, tolerate negative events, guide our children, find meaning in our lives. That wisdom can be found only inside ourselves. It comes from a higher force that approaches us through our dreams.

Freedom or Commitment?

I once knew a man who had a strange goal. He wanted to buy a desert island. His plan was to retire there and completely escape from civilization. When he came to me as a patient, he told me that this had been his goal for as long as he could remember. And it was crucial to him that he reach nirvana by his fortieth birthday. He didn't want one of those "ten years and then you die" types of retirements. "I want to live a long life in freedom," he insisted.

I could see that this man had no idea what freedom was. All his life he'd been looking for it in the wrong places. He was the only child of a mother who had grown up in poverty and felt she had never realized her potential. That wasn't going to happen to her son. He was raised "without limitations," he told me. If he didn't like one school, his mother let him transfer to another. If he had a fight with a friend, she'd find him a new one. If he didn't like a movie, they'd walk out and go to a different one. Her flexible attitude didn't have the intended effect on her son. He grew up to be a dreamer, lost in his own fantasies. He couldn't make plans or keep appointments. Decisions paralyzed him. If a friend invited him to come for dinner, he'd ask if they could check back with him an hour or so before it was served—he'd decide then. Needless to say, he had few friends.

He defined freedom as the ability to do whatever he wanted—whenever he wanted to do it—never closing off any options. "I'm not going to let life take my freedom away," he claimed. When I mentioned that growing up meant committing to things, and that adults make limiting choices all the time, his answer was that most people had "sold out." They'd fallen into the "trap" of adulthood, he felt, and the worst part of the trap was having to work. Only "suckers and slaves" worked all through life. That's where the desert island came in. There he'd be safe in his own world, without demands. When I met him, his dream was close to becoming a reality. The company he worked for had just gone public and he owned options that would enable him to retire if he lived modestly. He was thirty-seven years old, and all he had to do was wait out one year for the options to vest. But in that year, something happened that shocked him. He fell in love. He had always kept two or three girlfriends going at once so he'd have no temptation to commit. But one woman got under his skin. Now he faced a dilemma. If he wanted to marry her and raise a family, he'd have to keep working to earn enough money. No escape to paradise. His worst fear had come true—he was trapped.

But it wasn't the situation that was confining him.

He was trapped by the illusion that he could live without

demands or commitments, that it was possible to live a life that was stress-free.

Paradoxically, nothing creates more stress than the desire to avoid stress. This man was far from free. In the years before he came to me for therapy, he'd been so afraid of becoming trapped that he had panic attacks in elevators and planes. Now he found himself unable to take advantage of the best thing that had ever happened to him—the love of this woman. Even his fantasy of escape was impossible. (Living on a desert island doesn't exactly give you a host of options.) He couldn't begin living until he understood this truth—life is demanding. But if you meet life's demands, you get priceless rewards. You can create. You can have a sense of purpose. You can have deep relationships. You can feel passion. The illusion that we can avoid the demands of life keeps these joys out of our reach. Real freedom is the freedom from illusion.

Why is life so demanding? Because life is not a meaningless coincidence in a dead universe. Life is a higher force that moves with purpose. You may reach the point where you don't need to work for money. But to feel alive, you need some type of forward motion. Without it, you lose touch with life and fall into a meaningless existence. Then you're really dead inside, even if you're physically alive. We've all seen older people who are hunched over so badly they can hardly look up. Others are standing erect, full of life. Which do you think are still moving forward? Which are more free? As humans, we can only really live when we connect to higher life forces. Breaking this connection isn't freedom, it's a denial of our nature. If a fish could fly, that doesn't mean it's free, it just wouldn't be a fish. A fish is free when it can swim in the direction of its choice.

A deepened life force gives us inner freedom. My patient was looking for outer freedom. The more options, the freer he thought he'd be. This illusion made him obsessed with the things around him. It actually decreased his freedom. Look at the average materialistic person. Do they seem free? No amount of possessions or options can free us from the ultimate human limitation—time. Our supply is constantly running out. While trying to keep every choice open, we are wasting this most precious resource. Always waiting for something better to come along, we are paralyzed like a deer caught in headlights. That's hardly freedom. Inner freedom is the ability to move forward now. To do this you have to close off options. Time makes life demanding. You must choose because you don't have forever.

As obvious as this is, we have trouble applying it. Because each time you close a door, you suffer a little death. And it's human nature to try to avoid loss. But the result is more procrastination and wasted time. The trick is to change your experience of these moments of limitation. True, in an outer sense, you are giving up some opportunity or experience. But in an inner sense, you are actually gaining something. The life force doesn't come from the material world. Only when you give up your connection to the things around you will you find your life force. In that sense, you gain higher forces every time you give up something. The little deaths you suffer add up to more life.

Limitation has great power. The mythological symbol for this power is the Father. We are most familiar with the figure of Father Time with his hourglass and white beard. He symbolizes the inevitable—our fate, our death, and our ultimate helplessness. All of us, even little kids, react to this figure with a degree of fear. My patient had the illusion that the Father could not reach him on his desert island. Many people make an all-out effort to avoid the Father and his demands. All materialism is ultimately an attempt to avoid the Father. Not only is this impossible, it's a misunderstanding of the Father symbol. He is a threatening figure only when you resist him. When you submit to him, you get to share in his powers. This spiritual truth is portrayed in the New Testament story of Christ, the Old Testament story of Abraham and Isaac, and many other myths. There's a name for the correct relationship to the Father. It's called discipline. Every time you submit to the discipline of committing to one choice, you deepen your relationship to the Father. You are practicing the power of limitation.

Real freedom is being able to use this inner power. You aren't freed from the limitations of time, but you'll make the most of the time you have. You can feel this power in the following areas.

Relationships

Nothing weakens relationships more than the inability to commit. We wait for someone better, more magical. Real freedom is the ability to stop waiting and commit, knowing no situation can be perfect.

Mood

As strange as it seems, happiness is the celebration of outer limitations. There is a reason people from less industrialized cultures often seem happier than we are. They are less obsessed with what they can get from the material world. Real freedom, and the happiness that comes with it, is the ability to free ourselves from this obsession.

Events of Fate

In a mythological sense, the Father initiates all events. This means the events in your life have a higher meaning. This philosophy lets you accept even difficult events with grace and courage. Real freedom is the ability to learn from events rather than be their victim.

Creativity

Creativity comes from limitation. The more your outer world is limited, the more inspired you'll become to create something new, something that is not yet in the outer world.

Any art form—writing, for instance—goes better when you do it at a set time of day whether you feel like it or not—a limitation. As an artist, you are submitting to the Father. After a short time, you'll feel him help you create. And that is real freedom.

Rising Above Envy

I once worked with an up-and-coming young actress who kept stumbling over a career obstacle—her best friend. This other woman was also an actress, but one who seemed favored by destiny. My patient was terrific, but her friend was more glamorous. She didn't just attract some men, she attracted all men. The two women tried out for many of the same roles and without fail, this other actress was offered first crack at the best parts. "She's having the life I want," my patient used to tell me. She kept her jealousy under wraps until one TV-pilot audition season. The women were up for the same role on an ensemble show and, as usual, the friend got the part. But neither of them was happy. My patient could barely contain her envy. The friend wanted her own series and felt the role was beneath her. Then something happened that, looking back, must have been the hand of God. Before the first show ever aired, the friend was given the starring role in her own series. My patient was given her best friend's role on the show.

But that didn't solve things. My patient resented her friend more than ever. I reminded her that her wish had come true—she had stepped into her friend's life. But she felt she was getting hand-me-downs. Her envy became an obsession. She got to the point where she couldn't concentrate on her new role and almost lost the job. She was reacting like a child who breaks a new toy because it isn't exactly what she wanted. Finally, she ended the friendship and focused on her work. Her friend was hurt and mystified.

The season started, and her friend's show bombed and went off the air. My patient's show was a huge hit. She and her cast became big stars. But stardom wasn't what she thought it would be. She became obsessed with her appearance, jealous of her costars, and terrified of bad press. Worst of all, she wasn't enjoying acting anymore. Then she got a break. Her ex-friend called to congratulate her on her success. My patient told her, "Your life isn't as good as I expected it to be," meaning that she had taken the friend's old role and it wasn't what she'd imagined it would be. The friend, misunderstanding, said that in fact her life now actually was pretty good—since her public failure she'd felt less frantic and more connected to people. The conversation shocked my patient back to reality. She began to work to get back her life and her friend.

The reasons my patient was jealous are obvious. But why was she so unhappy when she got what she wished for? The truth is that contentment has nothing to do with what we do or don't have. Our happiness is dependent only on which world we choose to live in. There's the world where real life exists, and a lower world of lack. The choice hinges on our state of mind. Envy pulls us into the lower world. We envy what other people have—not just cars, houses, and money, but fame, beauty, and relationships. At the moment we envy a thing, we assume it's in limited supply. And in this world of scarcity it's natural for us to compete with one another. Imagine a party with six guests and only five pieces of cake. Someone won't be eating. My patient was pulled into this state because of her envy. And in it, she could trust no one. Her creative forces were blocked and she lost confidence in her acting. No amount of success could lift her out—she had to change her frame of mind.

We feel this world of flow and abundance inside of us. There's no scarcity in this place because higher forces enable us to create without end. Imagine the same party, but now each time someone takes a piece of cake, a new piece is created. Envy is not necessary—everyone eats all they want. But there's one catch—the higher world is moving. To keep up with it you have to continue to move forward in your own life. And the direction in which you move isn't random. Each of us has a preordained path through life. The path involves challenges, some very painful. We need the challenges to teach us to connect to something bigger than ourselves.

Because we are all different, we each have a unique path that will take us to this higher world. My patient's friend caught a glimpse of it after her show failed—that's when she discovered something bigger than her own ego. There's no way to logically prove that you're on the right path, but there is a way to live that allows you to sense its existence. The key is to train yourself to feel that whatever is happening to you right now is what's supposed to be happening, even if it isn't what you think you want. Each event in your life is personally meaningful because it belongs uniquely to you. This sense of meaning gives you the strength to then take the next step on your path, which is the only thing within your control.

Envy blocks our path because envy makes it impossible to experience meaning. When you envy someone, you are telling yourself you'd rather be on their path than your own. This makes your own path, and life, meaningless. It goes beyond coveting the things the person has. What really drives envy is the assumption that the other person is living in a different world, without the adversity and uncertainty you find on your own path. The objects they have—a nicer body, a bigger car, a better job—become magical symbols of their ability to live by a more favorable set of rules. But it's just an illusion. No human being, no matter what they have, is immune from adversity or uncertainty. Still, the illusion is hard to resist. We are surrounded by a degree of wealth unprecedented in human history. The result is an epidemic of envy that no one talks about. Even the newly rich are infected. They envy others who have even more than they do.

Envy can be more than an obstacle—it can be dangerous. Because when we fail to follow our own path, we lose our individual identity and suffer a spiritual death. There is only one force strong enough to make us let go of the people we envy and return to our own path. That force is love. The nature of love is that it accepts what is. If you send love to someone you envy, you're saying you accept that they have something you don't. You are reminding yourself that whatever they have is part of their path, and has nothing to do with you. You stop seeking satisfaction from things. All this comes from the simple act of sending love, which automatically puts you in the higher world. There's a sense of completion in the act of love that fills you up and relaxes your obsession with what you don't have.

The common objection to sending love to someone you envy is "But I don't like that person, so how can I send them love?" The answer is that love doesn't represent your approval of someone else. Love is a higher force that you can teach yourself to generate at will for your own benefit. The tool that allows this is called active love, which we have discussed. By the way, I use the word *active* because it takes effort to radiate love in circumstances where it doesn't come easily. First, it takes concentration to imagine love as a physical energy spread out in the world around you. Draw this energy in toward you and feel it concentrate right in your heart. The second step is called transmission. Send the energy from your heart toward an image of the person you envy. Feel the energy moving toward them. Hold nothing back. And remember that last, and most important, try not only to see the energy entering the other person, but to feel it enter. For a moment the love puts you at one with them. It's like closing a circuit—you'll feel a sense of flow as you enter the higher world. What someone else has won't concern you. You can let them go, get yourself back, and concentrate on the next step on your own path.

How to Love Yourself

A friend of mine is an acting teacher who has coached many of the biggest names in Hollywood. One night we were discussing why some actors go on to stardom while others, equally talented, do not. Is it the whim of the gods? Dumb luck? My friend claimed that if you showed him a group of gifted young actors, he could predict which ones would make it. I laughed and asked him when he'd become psychic. But he was serious—he believed there was one specific factor in actors' personalities that determined success or failure. The secret was how they dealt with auditions. Since I've had many actors as patients, I'm aware of how difficult it is to audition. You have to walk into a room full of strangers and bare your soul on cue. You're given five minutes to impress them, and believe me, they're not easily impressed. It's one of the hardest tasks in the world. No actors like auditioning, but some deal with it much better than others. According to my friend, the stars came from that group. All of them, he said, no matter how different they were, had one thing in common. It wasn't how well they prepared for their audition. The key was how they reacted after the audition was over. Unlike most of their colleagues, they never attacked themselves. Even if things went badly, they'd find some way to tell themselves they did okay. "They were missing the gene for self-attack" is how my friend put it. This made instant sense to me. Imagine a boxer who, when the fight is over, goes into the locker room and punches himself repeatedly in the face. That boxer won't want to fight much longer—the process is too intimidating. By being gentle with himself after an audition, the successful actor is already preparing himself for the next audition. He's working on the only variable he can control—his reaction to himself.

Modern life is one big performance. We measure ourselves at school, at work, with our friends, as parents. Social media makes it worse, slamming us with images of perfection. But few of us are like the successful actors my friend described. We judge ourselves viciously, and end up thinking we're not enough. When we make a mistake or lapse into a bad habit, we're trained to correct it by beating ourselves up. This just makes things worse. By the next day, we rebel against our own harsh standards. We respond like a teenager defying a stern parent, only we are the parent. Sure enough, our rebellion takes the form of the very behavior we judged so harshly the day before. It's an endless cycle.

Constant self-attack makes us feel secretly inferior, destroying the confidence to do new things. Most people accept this habit and the damage it does to them as "just the way I am." But it doesn't have to be. Anyone can break the destructive cycle by practicing what's best called self-love. We've all heard this term—it's constantly thrown around on Oprah-like shows and in self-help books. Frankly, it's always bothered me. The words seem saccharine and mushy, connoting a vague, feel-good state that's out of touch with reality. In my mind, self-love came under the heading of psychological loose talk—concepts that sound good but don't have the specificity to take you anywhere.

It's taken me years to discover what self-love really means. Now I realize it's the single most potent factor in human development. Self-love is the process of accepting the most inferior part of yourself. Anyone can accept the great parts, that's easy. The work is to accept the part of ourselves that we're ashamed of, the Jungian shadow, what he defined as the thing a person has no wish to be but can't get rid of. It might be your height, your ancestry, your college board scores, or the fact that you are an alcoholic. In the end the details never matter. Human beings have a fragile temporary place in the universe. It's natural for us to feel inferior. We try to hide this from the world—and ourselves— with a facade. We drive the right car, have the right body, send our kids to the right schools. But the moment the facade breaks down, and it always does, we attack ourselves. Self-criticism is our reaction to the failure to live up to our illusions about ourselves. But these failures are actually the most important moments in our lives—these are the times when our shadow breaks through. Mistakes and failures are supposed to trigger love. If we learn to love our shadow at these times we become whole and gain the confidence that comes from accepting ourselves.

Here's an exercise to help you break the habit of self-criticism and start loving yourself instead. The whole thing takes just a few seconds. First, try to imagine an inferior version of yourself, an alter ego that contains your every weakness and failing. Your shadow may look like a younger, needier image of yourself. Go back to a time in your life when you felt inferior, rejected, or insecure. Don't worry about what your shadow looks like. As you work with this, its appearance usually changes. The important thing is to make the image seem real, as if you're in the presence of a living being. If this being makes you feel uncomfortable, you're on the right track. Then accept this part of yourself unconditionally. Only love can do this. Feel your heart expand and send pure love to your shadow. If you have more time you can imagine hugging your shadow or reassuring it in words. The closest experience to this is when we comfort our children. We need to love ourselves with the same intensity. All this may sound hokey at first, but if you do this consistently, you'll be shocked at how real the experience becomes.

Self-love has the power to change everything in your life. You are less vulnerable to others' reactions. You are bolder and more relaxed. When you make a mistake, you recover much faster. But this power doesn't come easily. Understanding self-love, even using the tool a few times, does nothing. Self-love has to be practiced with great discipline. In California, where I live, there's been much criticism of the self-esteem movement in many schools. The critics claim the schools teach the kids that it's more important to feel good about themselves than to work hard, in effect, condoning a complete lack of standards. They may be over-stating their case, but they are right to object to self-esteem being sold as an alternative to discipline. The real practice of self-love is quite the opposite. Self-love and the resulting self-esteem cannot exist without discipline.

Self-love isn't giving up and telling yourself it's okay. That's denial. It means nothing to accept your failings if you make no effort in the first place. If you're too lazy to commit to life, you won't have the energy needed for real self-love. Self-love isn't self-absorption, either. In fact, narcissists can't accept and love their shadows at all. They need endless outer attention to reassure themselves that they don't have any failings. They have neither the courage to admit their weaknesses nor the discipline to learn to accept them. Narcissism is a form of spiritual laziness. All love, but particularly self-love, takes work. It requires real effort to learn to love the parts of yourself that you dislike.

The work of self-love reaps a tremendous reward—your heart opens. Your heart has powers that your head doesn't have. When you attack yourself, you are completely in your head, caught up in your judgments. That's a very limited world in which to live, and it gives you a limited view of your own potential. The heart runs on love, not judgment. Love knows no limitations—love gives you the power to do anything. If you have true self-love, nothing can stop you.

How to Stop Judging

Years ago, I worked with a not-so-young-anymore, aspiring film director. In his late thirties, he was still in the baggy clothes and shoulder-length hair he wore when the grunge look was cool. His career was as caught in the past as his appearance. Instead of spending his days developing story ideas, he'd aimlessly cruise the streets of Los Angeles and observe people. He found fault with just about everyone. He'd launch into a hypercritical inner dialogue about people's cars, appearances, manners, even the lives he imagined they led. Driving around, he felt completely alienated from this terrible world over which he sat in judgment. There was only one life about which he didn't have a strong opinion—his own.

His life wasn't going so well, however. He'd directed one film years before when he was still thought of as having potential. But that stage doesn't last long in Hollywood; there's always another new kid on the block. After his first film, he got several offers. He turned them all down, since none met the standard of greatness he associated with his work. Not only was he highly judgmental of every script submitted to him, he was also a vicious critic of the work of other filmmakers, especially if he considered them his rivals. The result was predictable; the offers tapered off. His friends and agents tried to reason with him, but he was determined not to compromise his "integrity." Years went by. Now he was no longer young and cool, just judgmental and isolated.

When he started therapy he was broke. He joked that he was in the "will direct for food" stage, but clearly he was desperate. He was even considering the unthinkable. For the first time in years he'd been offered a directing job and was thinking of accepting it. The job wasn't the meaningful film he saw himself doing. It was a teen horror flick— exactly the kind of movie he never missed a chance to vilify. In truth, he was lucky to get the offer, and he knew it. "But my world will fall apart if I take the job," he told me. "That's exactly what needs to happen," I responded. This man was living in a dream. He saw himself as a grand artiste in a special world. The reality around him could never meet this ideal; that's why he criticized it so harshly.

It is impossible to function in the world if you reject it. This man became crippled, unable to move forward, take risks, or even make a decision. On some level, we all have this vision of a world in which we're special, where every day is easy. It's a realm of illusion. It doesn't exist. We retreat to this fantasyland when we can't deal with reality. We become judgmental. And every harsh judgment is saying *I don't accept the world as it exists, I'd rather stay in my dream.*

HOW TO STOP JUDGING | 155

Judgment is based on fear. The universe is uncontrollable—things happen to us that we don't deserve and can't predict. But there is no alternate universe to which we can withdraw when things don't go our way. The ironic thing is that most of us think we're realists because we're so judgmental. Actually, our judgments come from the inability to accept life the way it is.

"Am I not allowed to have an opinion?" this man asked. Of course. There are all kinds of things in the world that aren't good—it's dangerous and unhealthy to deny that. But being judgmental goes beyond this. It implies that the thing shouldn't exist at all. When we think we know what should and shouldn't be in the world, we are playing God. We are saying our judgments should dictate the nature of reality, and that there's nothing higher than our thoughts. The moment we think we're that important, we lose sight of anything bigger than us.

When we judge, we cut ourselves off from life. The things we really need to know and the inspiration to carry them out come to us from a space beyond our ability to understand, from a space greater than our thinking minds. Being judgmental keeps us from this higher intelligence. In my own life, many of the things I've been most certain of have been wrong. Many years ago, I met a woman who I "knew" was bad for me. She was selfish, untrustworthy, conniving. I tried to avoid her, but she pursued me. A few months later, she introduced me to someone who turned out to be the closest friend I've ever had. Looking back, it's easy to see how a higher intelligence brought her into my life so I could meet this other person. But at the time, I was blinded by my judgments which I was sure were "right."

The film director had to learn the hard way. Among his other bad habits, he was especially critical of anyone he didn't consider an artist. But it costs a huge amount of money to make a movie, and the input of businesspeople is crucial as well. One of these nonartists was a studio executive of whom this director was particularly contemptuous. He didn't feel that the man understood his vision, and refused to speak to him. The executive, fearful of a director out of control, moved to have the man fired. I strongly encouraged the man to apologize to the executive, and maintain a daily, respectful relationship with him. He whined and complained, but since it was the only way to save his job, he overcame his judgments and treated the executive like a human being. When the film was finished, to his shock, he got another offer right away. It came from a friend of the executive, who was now singing the director's praises. "I guess I was wrong about him, and almost everything else," he said. This was his first step toward wisdom.

Judgment is what you already "know"—ideas inside your head based on past experience. These ideas we hold so dear let us feel that we're right, which turns out to be the ultimate booby prize. Wisdom has nothing to do with being right. It's the state where you can create the future with the help of an intelligence higher than your own. Our judgments keep us from this state.

The ancient Greek philosopher Socrates was told by the Oracle of Delphi that he was the wisest man on Earth. But Socrates was long convinced that the sum of all his knowledge was nothing. How then could he be the wisest man on Earth? Confused, he interviewed every wise man he could find, testing their knowledge. After years of this, he realized that indeed he was the wisest man on Earth. He was the only one who could admit that he knew nothing.

Giving up on being right takes a lot of work. Our egos are addicted to their self-importance. You have to interrupt your judgments at the moment you make them. Try it. Make a harsh judgment about someone right now. Feel how your mind knots up and shuts out the rest of the world. Now release the judgment. Feel your mind relax and your heart open. Let your heart expand even more. Feel the joy. Wouldn't life be better in this open state?

Staying on Track

An old client called me on September 14, 2001, three days after the attack on the World Trade Center. He wasn't reaching out because of fear or grief, although he felt plenty of both. He'd fallen into a lethargy and couldn't pull himself out. This was a real problem for him since he ran a company with over five thousand employees who were looking to him for leadership. "I just can't get myself to focus on business. It seems pointless." He was down on himself for his inertia but didn't know how to fight it. I told him his reaction was natural; people all over the country were having difficulty keeping their minds on their work.

"Do you think the criminals who attacked us have the power to physically destroy America?" I asked him. "Of course not," he said without hesitation. "Then what's their goal?" I continued. He thought for a moment. "To destroy our way of life," he answered. "And how could they do that?" I asked. The phone was silent for a few moments. "They could make us so distracted that we can't go on with our lives."

For most of us, evil is an overwhelming experience, especially when it takes us by surprise. Evil is a shock to our identities, making our everyday goals and activities seem meaningless. We're thrown into a stunned lethargy, our confidence gone. That, more than the physical deaths of the victims, was the end goal of those who attacked us. Unable to destroy us physically, their goal was to destroy our minds.

The world changed on September 11 not because of the magnitude of the disaster. It changed because we felt in our bones that the dangers we face have no end point, that we can't look forward to a time when the enemy is defeated and we can go back to feeling "safe." To a large extent, we had been protected from evil in America for a long stretch of time. September 11 forced us to accept the fact that evil is always going to be there. We can't react to this reality by just becoming angry and hopeless. We can't dream that evil is going to go away. We must accept the existence of evil and deal with it.

But why go on with everyday life when evil can strike at any time? The fact is, it's exactly because evil won't go away that we have to proceed in the face of it. If we wait for a time when we're safe from evil we'll have to wait forever. This has always been true but we've been able to deny it. We can destroy our attackers but we can't destroy evil itself.

Victory over evil comes only through changing our reaction to it. This is a spiritual issue. Once you look evil in the face it's impossible to go forward with life without some connection to higher forces. If evil inspires us to find these inner resources, then it becomes our spiritual teacher. This changes evil from a force that makes your goals feel meaningless to one that pushes you to achieve them. It makes you undefeatable as a person and, if we all can understand this, undefeatable as a nation. But if we don't develop a positive reaction to evil we become paralyzed.

How do we connect to these higher forces and become undefeatable? Prayer and worship are key. But there's something just as crucial—discipline. Discipline forms an invisible structure in your life, a structure that attracts and holds the higher forces. If spiritual forces are like fruit in an orchard, invisible structure is a box we use to carry the fruit home.

You can remind yourself of the power of this discipline box by drawing a square on a piece of paper. Draw a circle around the square, but not a smooth circle. Make it a squiggly line. Don't let this circle touch any part of the square. The square represents the invisible structure that discipline creates. The circle represents all the distractions in the outer world that can take you out of your discipline. They can be addictions to alcohol, junk food, TV, or the wrong friends. You can be distracted by obsessing on relationship conflict, finances, fear—anything that at the moment seems bigger than your path. When you keep the circle from touching the square, you are not allowing the outer world to destroy your discipline. The square is the source of unstoppable forces that take you toward your goals.

There are three kinds of discipline needed to stay on track. The first is called **structural discipline**. It consists of things you do routinely—eat, sleep, exercise, etc. The goal is to live in a constant rhythm. This connects us to higher forces because the universe functions in rhythm. Living each day with an organized structure teaches the ego to submit to something bigger than itself—time. To get out of a lethargic state, the first thing to do is put the structure back into your daily living.

The second type is called **reactive discipline**. It's the ability to control your reactions to the events that bombard you all day. If you're a sugar junkie and someone offers you a cookie, you need reactive discipline to refuse. If someone cuts you off in traffic, you need reactive discipline to keep from responding with rage. When you lose control, you've fallen under the spell of the outside world and lost connection with higher forces—which are only found inside.

Finally, you need to have **expansive discipline**. This refers to action steps you must force yourself to take to expand your life. In business this means reaching out to broaden your base of customers or connections. It also includes taking steps to develop new ideas and undertake creative pursuits. In personal life, expansive discipline includes making new friends or developing new activities. Because there's anxiety and uncertainty in doing new things, most of us avoid expansion. It takes discipline to consistently force ourselves into the unknown. The universe is constantly expanding. To stay connected to its higher forces, we need to keep up with it.

The rewards for living inside this discipline box are tremendous. Life is more meaningful. You can actually develop the strength to attain your goals. But most of us are still spiritual infants—we don't want to live in a way that's not easy. To get the perseverance to build the box we need to live by a new philosophy. Here are the spiritual virtues that are essential to moving forward in life today.

Humility

The ego likes big, dramatic actions that seem as if they'll magically change the future. This gives the ego a sense of power. Real discipline is quite the opposite. It's made up of an endless number of small steps, each of which can seem meaningless on its own. The ego has to humble itself to keep going on a productive course.

Anonymity

We all like to be acknowledged and applauded for each effort we make. In that sense we're like children needing parental approval every step of the way. This need makes it impossible to lead a disciplined life. The box is built from a million tiny steps, most of which go totally unnoticed by others. If you can't move forward anonymously, you become spiritually weak. Without the validation you crave, you'll eventually quit.

Ignorance

When we undertake things that take a lot of effort, it's human nature to want to know exactly what the reward will be and when we'll get it. Real strength is the ability to undertake a course of action without knowing what the results will be. The necessary spiritual attitude is "I just work here"—meaning your responsibility is to continue with the process independent of the reward.

Poverty

Material things, once built, last until they're destroyed. The box isn't a material thing. It consists entirely of your actions. No matter how disciplined you were yesterday, the box falls apart if you're not disciplined today. In that sense you wake up each morning with nothing. You are impoverished until you rebuild the box with your disciplined actions. Accepting this commits you to unending effort.

These principles give you the strength to move forward against great adversity. Just thinking about September 11 should inspire us to live by them.

Free to Stay, Free to Leave

I believe in marriage, though I couldn't convince my friend of that during a heated discussion we were having. He feels strongly that we're straying too far from traditional values. In particular, he maintains we've lost the sense that marriage is a sacred commitment. More than anything, he blames this loss on our reliance on therapy. "The shrink basically gives a person permission to bail out of their responsibilities." His tone made me feel personally responsible for the high American divorce rate. Counseling married couples is like doing counterterrorist work for the CIA, I explained. The successes are invisible and the failures get all the attention. I take great pride in helping people make their relationships work. The clients who decide after therapy to leave their relationships were often in situations that were abusive or unworkable from the start. In truth, those people could learn how to make marriage work only by leaving the ones they were in.

In practice, ideologies are not enough anymore. We live in a spiritual era that centers around free will. There is a tremendous drive to move forward as an individual. The spiritual progress of each person counts more than ever. People will no longer do things because someone tells them to. They want to live based on what they feel is personally right.

I can't convince people to work on their marriage. I can only help them get in touch with their own power. This power comes from developing a very specific personal quality. Paradoxically, this same quality also makes it easier to get *out* of a relationship and get over it quickly. And, sometimes, the only way to develop this power is to leave a relationship. The best name for this quality is emotional independence. It means you have a life and an identity that don't depend on anyone else.

Being emotionally independent doesn't mean you don't care about others or don't need them, just that you don't rely on them to give you things you can only give yourself. The easiest way to understand emotional independence is to study people who don't have it. A new patient will be referred to me because they can't get over the breakup of their marriage. I'll ask them when it ended and they'll say, "Five years ago." This is so common it doesn't surprise me anymore. These people are not feeling normal grief over the loss. No person in the world is worth wasting years of your life. They've lost something much bigger—themselves. They depended on their partner for an identity. Now that the marriage has ended, they feel like nobody.

As I've said, real identity requires constant forward motion in a painful and scary world. It's a big responsibility, too big for some to handle. These people see their partner as a magical figure who can create an identity for them, freeing them from the hard stuff. They put their own life on hold and center themselves on the other person like a moth circling a flame. Most harmfully, they confuse dependency with real intimacy. When they lose this magical other, it feels impossible to replace them. Actually it is, because no one has magical powers in the first place.

When someone like this enters therapy their predicament becomes an opportunity to develop emotional independence, often for the first time in their life. They usually accept this as the only way to get over their breakup, and because they're alone, they are willing to do the work. Then they make a surprising discovery. They find that the same independence they need to get over their last relationship is the best way to ensure the success of their next relationship. Their newfound sense of independence changes the kind of person they attract, the way they evaluate them, and the way they respond to them.

This comes as a shock at first. These people have tried to make their relationships work by giving up their independence. But look at how a dependent person functions in a relationship. Since they define themselves through their partner, they're hypersensitive to the partner's reactions. They try to control those reactions, usually by repressing themselves or by demanding too much, sometimes switching from one to the other. When this doesn't work they feel injured and either withdraw or attack. All this brings out the worst in the partner, creating problems. There's a lot of fireworks but little real connection.

It's independence that allows a real connection. A person with their own life and identity is less reactive to their partner. The relationship is important, but it's not life-or-death. This creates space between the two people—a kind of shock absorber—so conflict doesn't escalate so quickly. It's in this peaceful space that real intimacy happens. At the same time, the person's independence makes them more attractive. Nothing is more appealing than having a life of your own. Independence gives you something else, too—clear vision. When you need someone desperately your hopes and fears form a fog around them, keeping you from seeing who they really are. That's why people wake up in the middle of a bad relationship and ask themselves how they got there. Becoming independent is like cleaning an eyeglasses lens. All of a sudden you can see the world. You finally have a shot at picking someone with whom you have a realistic chance of making a marriage work.

The problem is, most people have no idea how to develop their own identity. You don't become independent by being angry, defiant, or hypercritical with your partner. Those are reactions that still center on the other person. Emotional independence is a process that requires work.

Handling Negative Emotions

The dependent person has no plan to deal with their own pain. The moment they feel an emotion that's unpleasant, they look to their partner to make it go away. This gives the partner too much power. Even when it works, it leaves the person feeling childlike and diminished. Independence means being able to deal with loneliness, hurt feelings, demoralization, and fear on your own. It doesn't mean you don't look to others for help, just that the first person you look to is yourself. There's a big difference between dumping your bad feelings on your spouse like unprocessed garbage versus trying to bring your feelings in control first and then asking for support. The first way provokes anger, the second, respect.

One reason people stay in bad relationships is they fear the pain that comes if they leave. As frightening as it is, facing this pain is a key step toward emotional independence. The secret to handling the pain of a breakup is to remember that it comes in waves. There are unbearable peaks when it feels as if the world is about to end. Remember, these moments never last. Knowing this teaches you to keep your perspective in the darkest moments, a skill that will serve you well for the rest of your life.

Usually your thoughts in these pain moments are not an accurate picture of what's really happening. It is not true that you'll never be with anyone else, that this was your fault, that the relationship could still work, or that it was a waste of time. These feelings are normal—they're a pull backward—and you need to label them and stop them on the spot.

Behavioral restraint is also necessary to end and get over

a relationship. This means using discipline in how you talk with your ex-partner and what you reveal.

Maintaining Personal Habits

When you handle everyday life with discipline, you create an invisible structure that can't be lost if a relationship ends. This includes your daily habits of eating, sleeping, exercising, and spending time alone. You can add to this the discipline with which you approach things you tend to avoid. These mundane habits are the foundation for an independent identity because they depend on no one but you. People without independence are quick to give up what little structure they have as soon as they get into a relationship—always a bad sign. The best way to maintain structure is to do a nightly review. It just takes two minutes. Note anything you should have done during the preceding day that you avoided, then make your commitments for the next day. Discipline is really a productive relationship to time, and it's a relationship you can't afford to lose.

Developing Outside Interests

Unconsciously, a dependent person wants to give up all interests outside of the relationship. It's part of seeing their spouse as that magical figure who will shield them from the world. Having a real identity means being responsible for your own forward motion through life, some of which needs to be outside the marriage. This includes things like friendships, service groups, hobbies, artistic activities. Your spouse should support what's important to you, even (and especially) if it doesn't involve him. If you meet someone who demands that you give up these interests, you're going to have problems.

Doing things that represent forward motion in your life is critical to keep from reconnecting to a person when a relationship is over.

Developing emotional independence is just the opposite of being self-absorbed. It requires having discipline and submitting to something bigger than yourself. With hard work, you can develop the power to get over the past, choose a good partner, and make a stable and lasting relationship.

Highly Motivated

For most of us, finding peace in today's world seems impossible. Stress follows us everywhere. As tough as life is, we make it more stressful than it has to be. We overwork, overschedule our kids, get into fights we could avoid. We follow the stock market too closely, watch every crisis on CNN, email each other frantically. It's as if we're addicted to living on the edge of chaos and disaster. Why choose to live inside a whirlwind? We don't set out to torture ourselves, although that tends to be the result.

We're addicted to stress because we don't know how to motivate ourselves without it. In the modern world, we look outside ourselves for everything, even motivation. Unless we're seduced or forced, frightened or enraged, we can't act. These energies cause tremendous stress. In the long run, they fail us, leaving us without purpose or direction. All that's left is the stress itself.

One of my patients was a striking example of this. She was a software designer who drifted through her twenties without direction or confidence. When she was thirty, she was hired by a dynamic man who had just started his own company. He saw her hidden potential and gave her more and more responsibilities and the promotions that went with them. Soon she was supervising many people and traveling around the world. This once timid, passive woman became a confident, creative dynamo. "I felt like I was shot out of a gun" was how she described it. I asked her how she had achieved this new state. "I didn't achieve it, I borrowed it," she said, meaning that she hadn't motivated herself. Her energy and direction were generated by her boss, sometimes through inspiration but more often through fear. "I didn't dare not be motivated. It felt like I had no choice." As the company grew, he demanded more and more until her stress level went off the scale. Then she quit.

At first she thought she was lucky. The stock market was still high and she cashed out her shares with enough money to not have to work. She set out to create a perfect life without stress. She married a guy who was the opposite of her boss, a college professor who rarely raised his voice. They had two kids, and lived in a beautiful house. She had plenty of help and free time. She was living her dream, but it wasn't working. That's when I met her.

She started therapy because her stress level was climbing off the charts again. She found herself picking fights with her husband over the smallest things. This gentle man was now screaming at her on a regular basis. The rest of her life was ruined by procrastination. She couldn't pay her bills until they were overdue, couldn't get showered and dressed until it was too late to be on time. Worst of all, she'd lost any sense of purpose and self-value, spending hours paralyzed in front of the TV.

She was completely confused. "I don't understand how this happened. I designed a totally new life, but I'm just as tense as when I was working. Except now, I don't even accomplish anything." It wasn't much of a mystery to me. She still had the same problem she started with—the inability to motivate herself from the inside. Anyone with this problem—and that's most of us—will look outside ourselves for energy and direction. She found them, temporarily, in the form of a driving, demanding boss who literally scared her into a high level of functioning. Without him, she had no motivation at all. So, unconsciously, she went about creating new outer stimulation. The fights with her husband, the demands of her friend, the fear of an unpaid bill—although these experiences were unpleasant, they sent surges of energy through her body. She was hooked on stress.

When you use outer stimulation to drive yourself, you are relying on what I call the lower motivational system (an offshoot of the lower channel I mentioned earlier). This woman used stress for motivation, but others get just as dependent on drugs, caffeine, the media, and even sex. It's a lower system because it comes from a passive, childlike part of us that avoids responsibility.

When your energy comes from outside yourself, you can't trust that it will see you through adversity. In the darkest moments, you lose your nerve and give up. This outside-driven energy comes in bursts, making you race around frantically but with little sense of real direction or accomplishment. Our culture is designed around this lower moti-vational system. Advertisements, fast food, smartphones pinging with text messages all suggest we can get whatever we need, right now. We're like lab rats, with no higher pur-pose, pressing the same levers over and over. The modern world has destroyed our will, but we're moving so fast we don't even realize it.

This loss of will is the central challenge for people today. Psychology usually skips over the will as if it is a superficial issue.

It's not.

A weak-willed person can never find herself. She's domi-nated by people and things around her, and loses touch with who she really is. Not only that, the stress she uses to motivate herself dooms her to a state of endless negativity.

Regaining your will is ultimately a spiritual issue. The part of you that can maintain its own course independent of outer distractions is your higher self. It connects you to those unstoppable higher forces that don't depend on things outside you. Only your higher self can give your life a sense of meaning.

You can activate your higher self with what I call the higher motivational system. It's a system that generates its own energy and that never stops moving forward no matter how difficult life gets. The secret of the higher system is to make every day you live, every action you take, personally meaningful. It is this sense of meaning that becomes your energy source.

To people today, the notion that meaning creates energy may seem strange. But we've all experienced it. Think back to a time when you helped someone you didn't know well. It may have been in just a small way, like giving up your seat on a bus. You weren't stimulated by fear or conflict, and there was no promise of immediate gratification. You did it because it felt right. It was meaningful. At that moment you were moved by a higher force.

The trick is to be able to create that sense of meaning, the feeling that there is a "rightness" to what you're doing, at every moment of the day. This gives you an inexhaustible source of will that doesn't need stress to trigger it and won't quit if you don't immediately get the results you want. You'll be calmer and more determined at the same time— the mark of the higher self. How do you create that sense of meaning? Being of service to others is part of it, but that won't help you move toward your personal goals. You create meaning by making everything you do during your day part of a plan that you've committed to in advance. Each act is meaningful because it represents a promise kept to yourself, which is why it feels "right." Small acts are just as meaningful as big ones.

The premise of a higher motivational system is simple, but the practice is difficult. It's human nature to get tired or distracted and go back to your old chaotic ways, and the stress that goes with them. You need a control panel to monitor the system and keep you on track. You can create this in the form of the aforementioned nightly review where, for five minutes before bedtime, you design your structure for the next day and put it into writing. First, the day needs an overall form. You want to have a clear idea of what you'll be doing in each part of it—when you'll eat, write, do errands, exercise, etc. You can challenge this if there's an emergency, but the goal is to stick to the plan as much as possible. This gives you the experience of literally creating your own day. You'll feel a sense of meaning as you move through each part of it. This is particularly important if you don't have a job to go to.

Next, pick at least one action you would normally tend to avoid and commit to it. If you can, even commit to the exact time you'll do it. When you take the action the next day, you'll feel the sense of having kept your commitment to yourself.

In a higher motivational system, the idea is to take action not merely to succeed, but because of the effect the action has on us. It connects us to higher forces, and changes our state from stressful to powerful.

A Separate Peace: Guilt and the Family

I worked with a woman whose father was making her sick—literally. Divorced, with a son away at college, she lived alone in a small apartment. Her father was in perfect health but, at age seventy, he decided he shouldn't have to take care of himself any longer. He came up with a simple solution—he'd move in with his daughter. He didn't tell her about his decision, he just began to show up unannounced. She'd get home from work and find him asleep on her living room couch. Soon he was there all the time. He stopped speaking to his friends or to other family members—she became the center of his world. If she went out nights or weekends, he'd pout like an abandoned child. As the weeks wore on he got more and more infantile, refusing to make his own meals or take care of his personal hygiene. Nor did he shop for the house or offer her any rent money. At first, she was sympathetic. Ten years earlier, he'd been depressed and medication had helped him. So she offered to take him to a psychiatrist and find him an apartment near her (which he could easily afford). He refused. He didn't want to help himself, he wanted to stay curled up on her couch. This man hadn't just taken over his daughter's apartment, he'd taken over her life.

Her reaction, although natural, disturbed her greatly. She began to hate her father. "Every time I come home there's this lump of bad attitude on my couch. All I want to do is go to my bedroom and lock the door. I don't even want to look at him." But as mad as she was, she felt powerless in the face of his passive resistance. She had no trouble standing up to her boss, but when it came to family members she had no strength. After a few months of this standoff she started to lose her health. It began with attacks of colitis, which she passed off as indigestion. But when her hair started to fall out in clumps, she had to admit she was in trouble. Still, when I met her, the first thing she asked me was how she could help her father. I suggested she forget about helping him for the moment. First, she had to deal with something in herself—guilt.

Both her parents were immigrants whose early years in this country were a struggle. Their four children were taught absolute loyalty to the family and told it was the only thing they could ever trust. The greatest sin was not to meet the expectations of a family member, especially the parents. My patient knew this was too extreme an attitude— she didn't teach it to her son. But when it came to her own father, she couldn't break free of her conditioning. She'd do anything he asked to avoid the crushing guilt of being a "bad daughter." When her mother died, his expectations became outrageous. Now she was stuck—too angry to submit to his demands and too guilty to say no.

"How do I get rid of the guilt?" she asked. I explained

that she couldn't make the guilt go away, at least not immediately. But she could do something more important—she could change her *reaction* to the guilt. Like most of us, when a family member made her feel guilty, her immediate assumption was that she'd done something wrong. She'd collapse and give in to their demands, just to escape the pain. The first step to healing herself was to feel guilty and *not* give in—in effect, to tolerate the guilt and do nothing. To reach that state, she had to first change the meaning of guilt. Instead of thinking that guilt was an indication that she'd done something wrong, she needed to look at guilt as a sign that she'd done something *right*.

To explain, I asked her why she hadn't conditioned her son the same way her parents had conditioned her. "Because I want him to move beyond me. I want him to be independent." Her son was lucky to have her as a parent because she was bestowing on him the greatest gift—his individuality.

Individuation is the process of growing up and separating from your family of origin. But in many cases, the family resists this process. The parents fear that if they allow a child to become her own person, she'll no longer be a loving and contributing family member. So they create a rigid set of expectations and train the child to feel guilty if she violates them. For people raised in this environment, guilt means they've had the courage to say no to the expectations of their parents and define for themselves what they think is right. Guilt means they're becoming themselves.

Painful emotions such as guilt can have a positive value. Instead of indicating failure, they can actually indicate progress. We've all experienced the physical version of this in the gym—your muscles hurt during a workout, but you give that pain a positive value because it's making you stronger. However, guilt doesn't always mean you've done something right. There's another kind of guilt that comes when you've violated your own standards of behavior. In that case, you *have* done something wrong, not based on the expectations of others but on your own sense of what's right. That kind of guilt is usually called a conscience. Paradoxically, you can't have real standards of your own until you've individuated.

Armed with a new tool, the woman began to say no to her father's demands. She'd immediately identify the guilt that came up as a reverse indicator and—for the first time in her life—she held strong.

When people go through this individuation process and learn to say no to their family members, they almost always fear they'll become cold or uncaring. They assume that once they are independent of their family, they'll become disconnected from them. This isn't true at all. The individuated person is emotionally free. That means they can choose to resist someone's demands and *at the same time* be loving toward them. They are separate, but still connected. In effect, they're giving out two different energies at once. These are the two basic energies in the universe—the one that separates us out as individuals and the one that connects us into a whole. This emotional ability to do two things at once is really the definition of individuation. Without it, every interaction becomes black-or-white—you either passively submit or you battle to the death. These black-or-white interactions are the source of the emotional and physical violence that occurs in families.

The secret of using both energies at once is to be emotionally proactive. Every time you have to say no, especially to someone close to you, balance it by taking the initiative to reach out to the other person. You can do this with your tone of voice, by touching them, or by taking a moment to explain your position (but not in a way that asks their permission). The love you express to them won't make you seem weak. When they feel your will to stay connected to them you'll actually seem stronger, even if they don't like the position you take.

The woman practiced this with her father. She stopped making every meal for him (he could easily do this himself) but instead of slamming her door and locking herself in her room, she'd make her own dinner and talk to him while she ate it. To her surprise, he began to be more respectful of her time and space. She kept this up in other areas, and within a month he'd gotten his own apartment. Her individuation had inspired him to grow up.

Becoming more of an individual can actually help your family. It makes perfect sense. When you're being yourself, your connection to the family is more real. Only what you give to others in free will has lasting value. The modern family has to evolve into a structure where everyone is free to be an individual and yet stays connected. Otherwise, the family unit will shatter more than it already has. This idea that the group needs the separate energy of each individual is obvious in the business world, where managers now consult with assembly-line workers to find out how to make their products better.

On the highest level, this is all an expression of our spiritual evolution. To oversimplify something profound, you can think of evolution as having three phases. In the first phase, the human race is one whole but no one has awareness of themselves as individuals. This is what the Bible calls the Garden of Eden. In the second phase, this collective organism splits into separate individuals, each of whom is now aware of himself but has lost his connection to his fellow men. This is expressed in the story of the Fall of Man. It's reflected today in the weakening of our social institutions—our communities, schools, and families. We've been reduced to a group of hyper-individualists, disconnected from one another. The final stage is yet to happen. Eventually, we will retain our individuality but come back together as a human family. In my mind, this is the goal of evolution—each person aware of their separateness and their connection at the same time. Since the work you do to individuate from your family requires these two opposing forces, it is a step toward this evolutionary goal.

This same process is playing itself out in our evolution as a country. We face many unprecedented, complex challenges. We can't be passive about them—that would be like the woman letting her father take over her apartment. But we can't overcome our many problems, geopolitical ones, for instance, without reaching out to the rest of the world family—which means showing some respect for their points of view, even if we don't agree. Just like someone individuating from her family, we have to learn to be proactive and inclusive at the same time. This will inspire the rest of the world. It's not a solution that lends itself to polemics—it won't satisfy people at the extremes—but it's the solution to the spiritual challenge we face.

I think our survival depends on it.

Acknowledgments

I was blessed to have the support of a group of talented people who were as enthusiastic about the book as I was. Each of them was crucial to its completion.

Many thanks to Barry Michels, Jamie Rose, Alicia Wells, Julia Stutz, Aline Garcia, Marisela Jimenez, Sarai Jimenez, Kristan Sargeant, Ben Greenberg, and Jennifer Joel.

ABOUT THE AUTHOR

PHIL STUTZ graduated from City College in New York and received his MD from New York University. He worked as a prison psychiatrist on Rikers Island and then in private practice in New York before moving his practice to Los Angeles in 1982. He is the subject of the Netflix documentary *Stutz*.